LEGENDS OF WARFARE

AVIATION

A-10 Thunderbolt II

Fairchild Republic's Warthog at War

KEN NEUBECK

SCHIFFER MILITARY

4880 Lower Valley Road   Atglen, PA 19310

Designed by Jack Chappell
Type set in Impact/Minion Pro/Univers LT Std

ISBN: 978-0-7643-5670-4
Printed in China

Published by Schiffer Publishing, Ltd.
4880 Lower Valley Road
Atglen, PA 19310
Phone: (610) 593-1777; Fax: (610) 593-2002
E-mail: Info@schifferbooks.com
www.schifferbooks.com

For our complete selection of fine books on this and related subjects, please visit our website at www.schifferbooks.com. You may also write for a free catalog.

Schiffer Publishing's titles are available at special discounts for bulk purchases for sales promotions or premiums. Special editions, including personalized covers, corporate imprints, and excerpts, can be created in large quantities for special needs. For more information, contact the publisher.

We are always looking for people to write books on new and related subjects. If you have an idea for a book, please contact us at proposals@schifferbooks.com.

Acknowledgments

This book is a labor of love by the author, who had a personal connection with the A-10 aircraft because he was a former Fairchild Republic Company engineer who worked on the A-10 program from the beginning of production in 1974 until the company closed in 1987. This book spans the history of the A-10 Warthog over two generations. The original project that spawned this book was a scrapbook of newspaper articles on the A-10 during Operation Desert Storm in the 1990s, which led to several writing projects over the years. The author thanks those who contributed to the book, including Anthony Abbot, Dave Conroe, John Gourley, John Golden, André Jans, Dennis R. Jenkins, Bryan William Jones, Ken Kubik, Niels Roman, Ton Smolders, and Josh Stoff. Organizations that helped include the Cradle of Aviation Museum and the Long Island Republic Airport Historical Society.

Abbreviations used in photo credits:
CAM = Cradle of Aviation Museum
LIRAHS = Long Island Republic Airport Historical Society
USAF = United States Air Force

Contents

Introduction

The experiences of the Vietnam War pointed out the need for aircraft that were dedicated to the mission of close air support (CAS). Although aircraft such as the A-1 Skyraider, the F-4 Phantom, and the A-7D Corsair were used in this role, they were not originally designed for this purpose. Thus, in March 1967, the US Air Force issued a request for proposal (RFP) to twenty-one companies for design studies involving a low-cost attack aircraft, designated as the A-X proposal. This resulted in a follow-on contract in May 1967 for more-detailed design studies, which was initially awarded to four companies.

In the meantime, the Air Force continued to refine the requirements for the A-X by using additional experience from Vietnam. The A-X concept was for an aircraft that would solely be dedicated to the CAS mission rather than compromising the performances of other new programs by making them take on additional roles of strike capability.

The final A-X RFP was issued in May 1970, with more-specific requirements that were added to the original speed requirement. The plane would have to be capable of carrying 16,000 pounds of maximum external load, of which 9,500 pounds would be in the form of ordnance.

Also, a head-on flying competition would be conducted for the first time in several years between prototypes built by the two finalists chosen by the Air Force. This requirement was added as a result of lessons learned from the difficulties in the development phase of the recent F-111 program.

On August 10, 1970, six companies submitted formal proposals for the A-X development contract: Boeing, Cessna, Fairchild Republic, General Dynamics, Lockheed, and Northrop. Of these six, the Fairchild Republic Company was probably the one company in the most precarious situation. The A-X program was to be one of the last new programs that would be issued, due to increased restrictions on Defense Department spending by a Congress weary of the Vietnam War.

The Fairchild Republic Company was created from the merger of the Fairchild Hiller Corporation and the Republic Aircraft Company in 1964. Both companies had long histories in the aviation field, with Fairchild having manufactured the C-119 Flying Boxcar and the C-123 Cargo aircraft, while Republic built major aircraft such as the P-47 Thunderbolt during World War II, the F-84 Thunderjet during the Korean War, and the F-105 Thunderchief, which flew in Vietnam. With the F-105 ending production in 1964, the combined company had no major aircraft in production at the time of the A-X proposal.

On December 18, 1970, Fairchild Republic and the Northrop Company were chosen as the two finalists by the Air Force. Each was to build two prototype aircraft and then participate in a competitive fly-off to win the A-X contract. Fairchild would receive $41 million for their development efforts, while Northrop would be given $23 million. The difference in the amount of money award resulted from a bold move on Fairchild's part, where they used the approach that they would be developing an aircraft that was representative of a production aircraft as much as possible. Northrop's approach was that of a conventional prototype, which would have required several changes before coming into production. This was a calculated risk that Fairchild was prepared to take, given that funding was very tight for a new development contract. Northrop would complain about the difference, but in the end they were stuck with the price that they quoted.

The fly-off was scheduled for early 1972, so there was only about one year for the aircraft to be designed and put together, a concept that was mind-boggling in comparison to aircraft programs of the early twenty-first century. In March 1971, the Air Force officially gave the designations of the A-9 for the Northrop aircraft and the A-10 for the Fairchild Republic version.

The author is seen here in front of an A-10 display during an open house family day event held at the Fairchild Republic Company in 1981. The author worked on the A-10 program as a reliability engineer at the time. *Ray Neubeck*

CHAPTER 1
A-10 Development

The A-10 was the most unusual-looking aircraft that was developed by Fairchild Republic for the CAS fly-off competition in 1970, and it was radically different in appearance than the conventional approach taken on the A-9 entry submitted by Northrop. The A-9 had shoulder-mounted wings, with engines located neatly in the fuselage under the wing, along with a single vertical tail fin.

The A-10, by comparison, had the two engines mounted high in pods that were mounted on the rear portion of the fuselage. The reason for this radical engine location by Fairchild was to increase survivability of the engines by keeping them away from runway debris and ground fire, as well as to function as a shield against ground infrared radar. The A-10 wings would be long and were perpendicular to the fuselage to provide the maximum amount of lift possible during takeoffs from short runways.

Additional survival features for the A-10 aircraft included the use of a 1-inch-thick titanium "bathtub" that would enclose the cockpit, providing protection for the pilot against ground fire as well as protection for critical flight control cables that were located in the cockpit area. The A-10 was essentially a plane that was built around the gun, which resulted in an off-center nose landing gear.

The fly-off competition between the two teams began in the spring of 1972 at Edwards AFB, California, refereed by the Air Force. Despite the different design approaches, the A-9 and the A-10 were close in performance, with both planes able to meet or exceed system requirements. The A-9 appeared to have better handling characteristics, but the A-10's radical design had the edge in maintainability and in the area of survivability. Cracks were discovered in the A-9 wing spar during flight testing. Also, some stalls occurred in the A-9 design, and there was a concern about the engine locations with respect to the creation of gases from the substitute 20 mm gun, causing flameouts.

On January 19, 1973, Fairchild Republic was announced as the winner of the fly-off competition. A major reason for picking the A-10 was that the A-10 prototype was made to be more representative of a production aircraft, and there would be fewer transitional difficulties in starting the production line. Fairchild's gamble of asking for more money for their production-ready design paid off.

Additional hurdles would occur before the A-10 production contract would be allowed to proceed. Members from the Texas congressional delegation pushed for the older A-7D Corsair II aircraft, built by Vought in Texas, to perform the CAS mission. Production funds were withheld and a new fly-off between the A-10 and the A-7 was conducted in April 1974 at Ft. Riley, Kansas, as mandated by Congress.

By May, it was determined by the fly-off pilots that the A-10 was the better aircraft for meeting the CAS mission, particularly in the area of target spotting in less-than-ideal conditions, as well as having better survivability features. The pilots would testify in favor of the A-10 to the House Armed Services Committee, and Deputy Secretary of Defense William Clements would testify in front of the committee that the fly-off results were unanimous in favor of the A-10. At this point, the A-10 production program was to proceed.

There was still one last challenge, which came in August 1974 from newspaper publisher David Lindsay, who lobbied Congress to use the PA48 Piper Enforcer for the CAS mission. This did result in some hearings in the House, but it was obvious that the Enforcer did not have the survivability features of the A-10, and the Air Force had no interest in the Enforcer for the CAS mission.

With this last challenge rebuffed, the A-10 finally had made it into the production phase. In some ways, the battles that the

A-10 would fight on the actual battlefields would be more straightforward than the fight in the political arena of Congress. Fortunately, for the interest of the United States, the A-10 program was able to survive these challenges in order to become an effective weapon system in the Air Force's arsenal.

The official designation for the six developmental aircraft and future production models would be the A-10A. At this time, the aircraft did not have an official name. Pilots would nickname the aircraft the Warthog due to its odd appearance. It was not until a few years later that a company-sponsored naming competition was held, with the winning name, Thunderbolt II, being chosen in honor of the original Republic-built P-47 Thunderbolt, which served in World War II as a fighter/bomber and ground attack aircraft.

The Fairchild Republic A-10 fly-off entry featured a radical design approach consisting of straight wings, dual vertical tail stabilizers, high-mounted engines, and nose landing gear located off-center to accommodate the gun. *Fairchild Republic archives via CAM*

The Northrop A-9 aircraft that competed in the A-X fly-off competition was a conventional approach that consisted of swept wings, a single vertical tail stabilizer, and engines that were mounted directly under the wings. This design approach for a CAS aircraft was actually adopted by the Russians for their CAS aircraft, the Sukhoi Su-25 "Frogfoot." *André Jans*

This is a very early artist rendering of what Fairchild Republic's CAS version would look like, circa 1968, prior to the A-10 designation. Note the elongated engine nacelle design and the lack of a cannon in the nose. Also note that the rendering shows the aircraft as a two-seat aircraft and that there are only two wing pylon weapon stations under each wing. *Fairchild Republic archives via LIRAHS*

This is a later artist rendering of Fairchild Republic's A-10, circa 1970. At this point, the wing pylon weapon stations have increased to four stations under each wing, plus three pylons under the center fuselage. The nose design at this point did not show the cannon protruding as much. *Fairchild Republic archives via LIRAHS*

In 1974, the A-10 had to undergo a second fly-off competition with the A-7D Corsair, which was used by the Navy and the Air Force. *USAF photo by TSgt Frank Garzelnick*

The PA48 Piper Enforcer was briefly considered by Congress for the CAS role in 1974, but it did not meet CAS requirements and was not accepted by the Air Force. It is actually a predecessor for the concept of light attack aircraft being developed after 2010. *USAF*

At the Fairchild Republic plant in Long Island, New York, the first A-10 prototype aircraft had engine ground testing of the General Electric TF34 turbofan engines in late 1971. *Fairchild Republic archives via CAM*

Workers load the fuselage of the first A-10 prototype into a C-124 transport aircraft for the trip to Edwards AFB, where it would be reassembled and commence with flight testing in May 1972. *Fairchild Republic archives via CAM*

The first A-10 has been made ready for shipping to Edwards AFB from Long Island in early 1972, via a C-124 transport aircraft. *Fairchild Republic archives via CAM*

The second A-10 prototype aircraft is being assembled at the company's plant in early 1972. It would join the other A-10 prototype at Edwards and begin flight testing in July 1972. *Fairchild Republic archives via CAM*

The first A-10 prototype aircraft, tail number 71-1369, made its first flight at Edwards AFB in May 1970. The two A-10 prototypes would accrue over 328 flying hours. *Fairchild Republic archives via LIRAHS*

CHAPTER 2
A-10 Details

The most-defining feature of the A-10 is the 30 mm cannon that protrudes from the nose of the aircraft. The development of the 30 mm cannon was a separate contract that was conducted by the US Air Force. Extensive studies were conducted by the Air Force in determining the optimal shell diameter that could be fired from an aircraft. Included in these studies was the experience of a World War II German *Stuka* pilot, Hans Ulrich Rudel, who used a 30 mm equipped J-87 *Stuka* to destroy over 500 Russian tanks on the eastern front. Rudel worked with Pentagon engineers during the original A-X program development, and he stressed the importance of a slower-moving aircraft for firing the gun in order to achieve greater accuracy. The 30 mm shell size was determined to be optimal for maximum penetration for the A-X.

To get the maximum gun performance, an old design was chosen, that of the Gatling gun, which was developed in 1860. GE won a "shoot-off" with Philco to win the A-10 gun contract. GE had experience with implementing Gatling gun design into aircraft going back to 1946, and more recently with the F-104 and F-105 aircraft. The 30 mm cannon was installed into the A-10 in 1975 and is designated as the GAU-8/A.

It was noted that since the aircraft would be moving while firing, it would be impossible for two consecutive shells to be fired from the same point. Thus, a requirement for a high rate of fire was employed, and this led to the modification of the Gatling gun design. The new design for the cannon would use seven rotating barrels that could accommodate the high rate of fire at the rate of seventy shells a second. Shell design would be of two types, one that had depleted uranium in the tips of the shell, which had high density for maximum armor penetration, and another shell type that had high explosives in the tip.

The A-10 was essentially a plane that was built around a gun. The gun assembly consisted of seven long barrels and was almost 20 feet long, which included a very large ammo drum that had to be fitted in the forward fuselage. Fairchild Republic engineers took a novel approach with regard to the nose landing gear of the aircraft, by locating it off-center of the fuselage centerline in order to accommodate the long barrels of the gun and allow the landing gear to retract into the fuselage. The gun could fire at a slow or high rate of speed, with the maximum rate being 4,000 rounds per minute. The ammo drum could hold 1,350 rounds, so in theory all rounds could be expended in less than a minute if the trigger was held for that long!

The A-10 would be powered by a pair of General Electric TF 34 turbofan engines. Fairchild Republic chose the GE engine at the time because it was believed that it was more developed and had better maintenance features. The GE engines consisted of four stages and used titanium fan blades. *Fairchild Republic archives via CAM*

The major feature of the A-10 aircraft was the GAU-8/A 30 mm cannon built by General Electric, which the aircraft was built around. *Ken Neubeck*

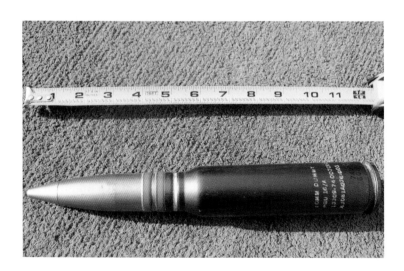

The 30 mm shell used for the GAU-8/A. The shell shown here is inert, with a dummy tip that is used for practice. Typically, the tip consists either of depleted uranium or high explosives. *Ken Neubeck*

The 30 mm GAU-8/A Avenger cannon system is almost 20 feet in length. The complete gun system is seen here at an air show exhibit, removed from the A-10, with the full complement of 30 mm shells that would be carried in the ammo drum seen on the right of the photo. *Ken Kubik*

Ground crew from the 104th TFG ANG unit are removing 30 mm shells from an ammo bucket into an automatic loading car that will load the shells into the ammo drum of the cannon, which has a 1,350-round capability. *Ken Kubik*

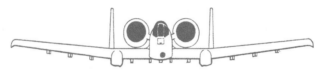

STORE	Kg	11	10	9	8	7	6	5	4	3	2	1	TOTAL MAX
MK-82 LDGP – GENERAL PURPOSE BOMB	240	1	1	3	3	6	6	6	3	3	1	1	28
MK-82 HDGP – GENERAL PURPOSE BOMB	249	1	1	3	3	6	6	6	3	3	1	1	28
MK-84 LDGP – GENERAL PURPOSE BOMB	894			1	1	1	1	1	1	1			6
SUU-25 C/A FLARE DISPENSER	224		1	3						3	1		8
LAU-68 A/A ROCKET LAUNCHER	110		1	3	3	3	3	3	3	3	1		20
LAU-68 B/A ROCKET LAUNCHER	120		1	3	3	3	3	3	3	3	1		20
MK-36 MOD 1,2,3, DESTRUCTOR BOMB	254	1	1	3	3	6	6	6	3	3	1	1	28
MK-20 MOD 3 (ROCKEYE II) DISPENSER	216	1	1	3	3	6	6	6	3	3	1	1	28
CBU-58/B DISPENSER SUU-30	372	1	1	3	2	2	6	2	2	3	1	1	20
CBU-71/B DISPENSER SUU-30	372	1	1	3	2	2	6	2	2	3	1	1	20
CBU-52 A/B, B. B/B DISPENSER SUU-30	356	1	1	3	2	2	6	2	2	3	1	1	20
AGM-65/A MAVERICK MISSILE	210			3						3			6
SUU-23A 20 MM GUN POD	789					1		1					2
MK-82 LASER BOMB GBU-12/B, A/B	295	1		1	1				1	1		1	6
MK-84 LASER BOMB GBU-10/B, A/B, B/B	934		1	1					1	1			4
MK-84 EO – TV GUIDED BOMB GBU-8/B	1027		1	1					1	1			4
SUU-20 A, A/A, A/M, B/A, TRAINING DISP.	125				1	1		1	1				4
BDU-33B, A/B, B/B – PRACTICE BOMBLET	11			3	3	6	6	6	3	3			24
600 GAL FUEL TANK	1887			1		1		1					3
MER-10N – MULTIPLE EJECTOR RACK	100				1	1	1						3
TER-9A – TRIPLE EJECTOR RACK	42		1	1	1	1		1	1	1			6
LAU-88/A MAVERICK LAUNCHER – TRIPLE	210			1						1			2

In addition to the gun, the A-10 was designed to carry a significant amount of ordnance under the wing and the fuselage. In all, there were eleven weapon stations: four under each wing and three under the center fuselage. Ordnance carried by the A-10 included the Mk. 20 Rockeye cluster bomb and the AGM-65 Maverick missile. Thus, the A-10 aircraft was capable of carrying more bombs than the World War II B-17 bomber, or the Republic F-105 Thunderchief. *Fairchild Republic Archives*

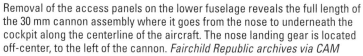

Removal of the access panels on the lower fuselage reveals the full length of the 30 mm cannon assembly where it goes from the nose to underneath the cockpit along the centerline of the aircraft. The nose landing gear is located off-center, to the left of the cannon. *Fairchild Republic archives via CAM*

The cannon's ammo drum is located at the top of this photo, and it interfaces with a feed mechanism that takes the shells from the drum and feeds into the gun barrels. The cannon assembly was made by General Electric of Massachusetts. *Fairchild Republic archives via CAM*

The TER-9/A triple ejector rack was used on the A-10, and it holds three bombs and can be mounted to one of the existing pylon stations underneath the center fuselage. *Ken Neubeck*

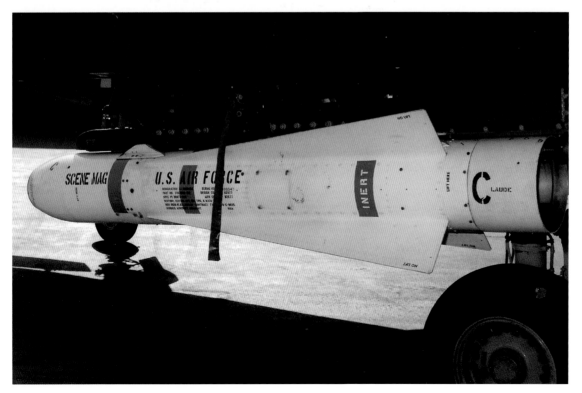

One of the major weapons used by the A-10 is the infrared guided AIM-65 Maverick missile, which can be carried under different wing pylon stations. *Ken Kubik*

The A-10A cockpit features standard round flight gauges that are located on the main console. The heads-up display (HUD) is located on top of the main console. The Armament Control Panel is located on the lower left of the console, while the TV Monitor is located on the lower right. *Fairchild Republic archives via CAM*

The control stick is located directly behind the fuse panel in the cockpit, and it contains rudder control functions. The stick contains buttons located in different areas on the top part of the stick for weapon release, as well as the gun trigger switch, which is located on the side of the handle for the pilot's thumb. *Fairchild Republic archives via CAM*

Located on the left console is the engine throttle quadrant, which consists of dual handle control for each engine. Located immediately in front of the quadrant is a panel containing a series of emergency switches for controlling trim, speed brakes, and emergency weapon jettison. The knob on the far right of the photo is the landing-gear actuation handle. *Fairchild Republic archives via CAM*

FLIGHT DATA STOWAGE

The right console contains a flight data stowage bin that is used for storing maps and other paperwork. The aircraft lighting-control panel is located forward of the bin, and it controls both interior and exterior aircraft light. There is a portable cockpit lamp that is mounted on the inside that the pilot can use for reading maps. *Fairchild Republic archives via CAM*

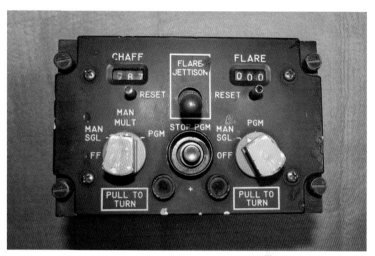

One of the instruments used in the cockpit is the control box for the AN/ALE-40 chaff-and-flare dispenser. The construction of this box is similar to the construction of other control units that are located in the cockpit, where it makes use of analog counters, control knobs, push-button switches, and toggle switches. The panel contains internal lighting. *Ken Neubeck*

The A-10 has an unusual landing-gear layout in that the nose landing gear is located on the starboard side of the centerline of the fuselage in order to accommodate the 30 mm cannon installation. The left and right main landing gears have a pod that is installed into each wing. *Ken Neubeck*

Dispenser units for the chaff and flares are located in four areas underneath the aircraft—under both wing tips and in the rear portion of each main landing gear. Each dispenser can be loaded with thirty chaff cartridges or flares, which are used to defend against enemy missiles. *Dennis R. Jenkins*

Ground refueling is accomplished through a quick-access area located on the portside main landing-gear pod. The fueling probe goes into the entry point seen on the left side, and controls are accomplished through a panel located to the right of the entry point that consists of indicator lamps, toggle switches, and push-button switches. *Ken Neubeck*

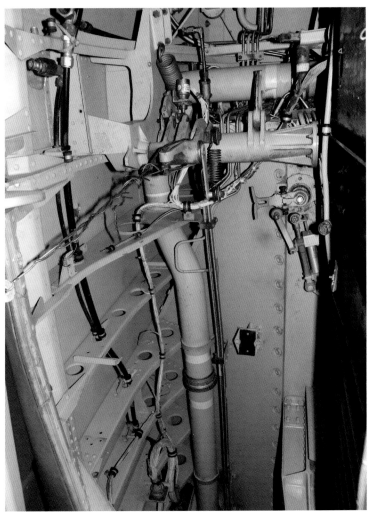

This is the inside of the nose landing-gear well. The large pipe that is located on the ceiling is the fueling line that goes from the Universal Aerial Refueling Receptacle Slipway Installation (USARSI) to the main fuel tanks. The turning links for the nose landing gear are located at the top of the well. *Ken Neubeck*

Aerial refueling is accomplished through the in-flight hookup with a tanker aircraft, which extends the probe into the top area of the A-10's nose, where an access door slides open to reveal the USARSI, as seen here with an early A-10 aircraft. Aerial refueling allows the A-10 to perform long-duration missions lasting four hours or more. *Fairchild Republic archives via LIRAHS*

This airborne shot of an A-10 in action illustrates the unique straight wing and dual tail section of the aircraft. The straight-wing design allows the A-10 to perform a tight turning radius. The unique dual vertical stabilizer tail assembly proves stability during severe banking maneuvers.
USAF photo by SSgt Michael Battles

Both the pilot and the cockpit equipment are protected from ground fire by a 1-inch-thick titanium bathtub that surrounds them. *Fairchild Republic archives via CAM*

A Fairchild Republic worker is installing ballistic foam pieces into the fuel portion of the wing sections. The foam soaks up fuel inside of the wing and reduces the possibility of fire from shell impact. *Fairchild Republic archives via CAM*

The A-10 was the first USAF twin-engine aircraft that has interchangeable engines. The engines are located high on the fuselage to lessen the impact from ground fire during combat or impact from ground debris on unimproved runways. *Ken Neubeck*

At Edwards AFB in August 1976, tests were conducted on the new ACES II ejection seat as installed into a custom, rocket motor-powered sled that rides on a rail system. *Fairchild Republic archives*

This test sequence shows the dummy being ejected from a moving test sled at zero altitude. *Fairchild Republic archives*

Initial A-10 aircraft were outfitted with the ESCAPAC seat system, but the ACES II ejection seat system would soon be employed. With the points located on the top of the headrest, the ejection seat was capable of going through the glass canopy in the event the canopy did not eject properly. *Fairchild Republic archives via CAM*

CHAPTER 3
A-10 Production

It had been more than ten years since the final assembly area in the Fairchild Republic plant had been busy, and that was when the last F-105 Thunderchief rolled out in 1964. There was some concern by the government during the A-10 Critical Design Review (CDR) that was held in May 1974 regarding Fairchild's production readiness.

Among the concerns was the significant gap between production programs and the inexperience of the current management in this area. Additionally, the machines in the plant that were used to fabricate parts were over twenty years old and required updating. The production plan that resulted was to build most A-10 subassemblies in the Fairchild Republic Farmingdale (New York) plant, as well as some subassemblies in the company's Hagerstown (Maryland) plant, with the latter being the location for final assembly and flight testing prior to final aircraft sell-off to the Air Force.

The A-10 production line would start with all six development, test, and evaluation (DT&E) aircraft being built entirely at the Farmingdale plant. In late 1974, the first DT&E aircraft were assembled and then taken apart for transport by a C-5 aircraft to Edwards Air Force Base for assembly and flight testing. The second DT&E aircraft would be the first A-10 aircraft to actually fly out of nearby Republic Airport.

Each DT&E aircraft would be used for a different test or evaluation, from aerodynamic studies to weapons and systems testing to climate testing. These aircraft would be available for later in the production programs when problems and need came up. In addition to these six aircraft, there would be two airframes built for static and fatigue testing, with the latter being tested in the Farmingdale plant.

After the DT&E aircraft, the first four production aircraft were built entirely at the Farmingdale plant and eventually were sent to Edwards AFB for additional testing. From that point on, production work was divided equally between the two plants, with the Farmingdale facility doing all the subassembly work for the fuselage and wing sections, and the tail assembly being assembled in Hagerstown. After completion of the subassemblies in Farmingdale, they were trucked down to Hagerstown for final assembly with the tail section, and eventually for company flight testing prior to individual aircraft sell-off to the Air Force. By having two locations in two different states, this would help politically in providing a base of support from each state's congressmen.

A number of decisions were made by Fairchild Republic that would aid in keeping production costs down and the A-10 production line running smoothly. A design-to-cost approach was used, which meant that the aircraft design used simple construction techniques that kept tooling costs down. Rivet construction was the main technique for assembling the different panels and skin structures to the frame of the A-10 aircraft. Standard conical or flat shapes were used for skin surfaces and panels, thus preventing the need for any elaborate sheet metal formation. An example of this is the engine nacelle design, where a cylindrical shape was used in lieu of the teardrop shape that was used in other military aircraft.

The aircraft was unique in the Air Force, since it had a large number of interchangeable components between the left and right sides of the airframe. Components of the fins, rudder, main landing gears, wing panels, fuselage sections, and pylons were interchangeable, as were the two engines, making the A-10 the first Air Force twin-engine aircraft on which the engines could be interchanged. Using interchangeable components was a major aid in keeping spares costs under control.

With the startup of A-10 production, there were some growing pains that had to be endured for the program, since it had been more than ten years since the last major aircraft production program, the F-105, was in the Fairchild Republic plant. Since that time, the company had dropped to under 1,000 employees by the time that the A-10 program had been awarded. A hiring program took place as production began, both for the subassembly location in Farmingdale and the final assembly in Hagerstown. The number of employees for both locations would eventually reach close to 10,000. Fortunately, the company had been able to retain many of their top-level engineers from the previous F-105 program.

Initial paint schemes ranged from the light gray for the two prototype aircraft to the gunship gray that was used on the first DT&E aircraft. Early-production A-10 aircraft were painted in an asymmetrical gray-and-white pattern combination, consisting of a medium gray on the upper part of the fuselage and a lighter shade of gray, called a ghost gray, on the lower fuselage. In addition, painted on the lower forward fuselage was a gray ellipse shape to simulate the canopy, as a distraction for enemy gunners on the ground trying get a fix on the aircraft from below.

A-10 production aircraft at the Fairchild Republic plant in Hagerstown are being prepared for final sell-off to the Air Force. The aircraft on the right has both the crew- and maintenance-boarding ladder deployed. *Fairchild Republic archives via CAM*

The Fairchild Republic plant located in Farmingdale, Long Island, New York, circa 1970. *Fairchild Republic archives via CAM*

The final assembly area for the A-10 fuselage was located in the center of the main building of the Farmingdale plant in an area designated as Broadway. Each group of A-10 assemblies was sequential in serial number. In the final assembly area in Farmingdale, each wing assembly would be paired with the fuselage and engine assembly for that aircraft. *Fairchild Republic Archives via CAM*

This is the Farmingdale plant at peak production. Production ran from 1975 through 1984, with the maximum production rate that was achieved on the A-10 program being thirteen aircraft a month. *Fairchild Republic Archives via CAM*

The wing assembly for each A-10 production aircraft was built at the Farmingdale plant and would be matched up with a fuselage section. Then the two sections would be transported to the Hagerstown plant in Maryland. This would be done for over 700 aircraft, since there were a few early-production A-10s that flew out of the Farmingdale plant. *Ken Neubeck*

Each completed A-10 fuselage section (front and rear) and the wing section would be transported by individual truck from Long Island through the New York City area down to Maryland. *Fairchild Republic archives via Cradle of Aviation*

The final assembly area for the completed A-10 aircraft was located in the main building of the Hagerstown plant, where the wing and the engine nacelles were mated with the fuselage. After assembly, final checkouts were performed and then flight testing would be conducted prior to sell-off to the Air Force. *Fairchild Republic archives*

The final production line of fully assembled A-10 aircraft was located in a large hangar in the Hagerstown facility. Aircraft are fully assembled, with both the engines and gun installed. The next step is painting, and then flight testing. *Fairchild Republic Archives via CAM*

One of two General Electric TF34 turbofan engines is ready to be shipped with associated fuselage to Hagerstown. *Ken Neubeck*

The first DT&E production aircraft, tail number 73-1664, was transported in sections from the Farmingdale plant to Edwards AFB via a C-5 transport that landed in Republic Airport in late 1974. The aircraft would conduct various tests at Edwards. *Fairchild Republic archives via CAM*

The first DT&E A-10 was painted in gunship gray, and after arrival at Edwards AFB it was outfitted with a substitute 20 mm cannon during flight testing at Edwards AFB, since the 30 mm cannon design was still being finalized by General Electric. *Fairchild Republic archives via CAM*

The first DT&E A-10, tail number 73-1664, had the number "1" painted on its tail, signifying that it was the first production A-10. This aircraft was very active during its lifetime, with early testing conducted at Edwards; later it would be converted to the N/AW two-seat evaluator. *Fairchild Republic archives via LIRAHS*

Early-production A-10 aircraft would be painted in a two-tone light-gray scheme to allow it to blend in better with the sky. As part of this paint scheme, a false-canopy shape in dark gray would be painted on the lower nose section fuselage. *Fairchild Republic archives via LIRAHS*

The second DT&E aircraft was the first A-10 to fly out of the Farmingdale plant, and it is seen here landing at Republic Airport in 1975. This aircraft was one of the first A-10 aircraft to be painted in a two-tone light-gray scheme. *Fairchild Republic archives via CAM*

The fourth DT&E A-10 aircraft, tail number 73-01667, was used for gun testing early in the program and was later used for testing during the gun gas ingestion investigation. It was nicknamed "Lucky Seven." *Fairchild Republic archives via CAM*

Lethality testing of DT&E A-10 aircraft was conducted at the gunnery range at Nellis AFB in October 1975. Targets included retired US tanks and captured T-62 tanks. *Fairchild Republic archives via LIRAHS*

This particular T-62 tank target located at the gunnery range at Nellis AFB shows the results of several 30 mm shell hits from a single A-10 pass during lethality testing that was conducted in October 1975. The A-10s that were used in this test were DT&E aircraft. *Fairchild Republic archives via CAM*

A-10A Specifications

Wingspan	57.5 feet
Length	53.3 feet
Height	14.6 feet
Empty weight	24,000 pounds
Maximum weight	50,000 pounds
Power plant	Two TF34-GE-100 turbofan engines
Maximum speed	439 mph
Cruise speed	340 mph
Service ceiling	45,400 feet
Ferry range	2,500 miles

A-10 Aircraft Program History

A/C Type	Quantity	FRC S/N	AF Tail Number	Current Status
Prototype	2	Proto 1, Proto 2	71-1369 through 71-1370	Inactive
DT&E	6	1 through 6	73-1664 through 73-1669	Inactive
Production	52	7 through 58	75-0258 through 75-0309	Inactive
Production	43	59 through 101	76-0512 through 76-0554	Inactive
Production	100	102 through 201	77-0177 through 77-0276	Inactive
Production	144	202 through 345	78-0582 through 78-0725	Inactive
Production	144	346 through 489	79-0082 through 79-0225	80% Active
Production	144	490 through 633	80-0140 through 80-0283	Active
Production	60	634 through 693	81-0939 through 81-0998	Active
Production	20	694 through 713	82-0646 through 82-0665	Active
TOTAL	**2 prototype aircraft, 713 production aircraft**			

CHAPTER 4
Initial A-10 Base Deployments

As the A-10 started making its way into service in the US, it would receive enthusiastic responses from many of the pilots who were assigned to fly the aircraft. The ground support mission was a unique concept for the Air Force, along with the arrival of a unique aircraft to meet that role; the A-10 would draw a lot of attention from pilots. These pilots preferred the mission of flying just above the treetops, as opposed to those pilots who wanted to fly high and at speeds exceeding Mach I.

Like any new aircraft that is initially deployed, there was a learning curve for the pilots to get used to the nuances of the new A-10 aircraft. Such nuances required the need for pilots to be vigilant when flying at low altitudes, very close to the ground, and to be aware of surroundings such as trees and mountains, particularly when engaging a target. As a result, there were some incidents that occurred during the early stages of the program that demonstrated the need for ground collision avoidance.

In April 1978, when the 100th A-10 aircraft was delivered, the Air Force used the occasion to officially designate the A-10 aircraft as the Thunderbolt II. It honored the P-47 Thunderbolt aircraft that had been built by Republic Aircraft Company during World War II. Despite this official name, the unofficial name, "Warthog" or "Hog," in honor of its ungainly appearance, was used by many pilots who flew the aircraft.

As more and more A-10 aircraft were being deployed at different bases, the aircraft were subjected to a series of operational tests, beginning in 1977, that would test its ability to fly multiple sorties in a single day with minimal turnaround time. One such test was held at RAF Bentwaters (United Kingdom) in April 1980, where a fleet of eighty-nine A-10 aircraft flew 579 hours during 533 sorties in fourteen hours, for a one-day sortie rate of almost six.

In 1978, a special milestone was reached when the 100th A-10 was delivered to the Air Force. Also, in June 1978, the first combat-ready A-10 wing, the 354th Tactical Fighter Wing (TFW), was established at Myrtle Beach, South Carolina, a process that took place five months sooner than originally planned. In December 1978, an A-10 from Davis-Monthan AFB became the first A-10 to go over the 1,000-hour flying mark.

The first A-10 delivered to the Air National Guard (ANG) was to the 103rd Tactical Fighter Squadron (TFS) at Bradley AFB in Connecticut in May 1979. Within a short amount of time, three other ANG bases would be activated in Massachusetts, New York, and Maryland with A-10 aircraft, thus making a total of four; A-10s that were based in Bentwaters would make many trips to US-supported bases in Ramstein and Spangdahlem in Germany.

By 1980, with deployment in Europe, there was a change to the A-10 Warthog's appearance, with a lizard-style camouflage paint pattern involving medium green, olive green, and gunship gray, which was developed to allow the A-10 to blend in better with the European environment. The paint scheme would be given the official name of European I and be used for another decade.

Shortly after the A-10 was deployed in Europe, it was determined that the pilot workload was very high and that additional navigational aids would be required. Frequently, the pilot would be flying low in the hilly and tree-lined European environment and would have to read road maps to identify landmarks, while at the same time avoiding the terrain. The addition of an inertial navigation system (INS) along with a radar altimeter would improve the pilot's workload. The change would be retrofitted throughout the entire fleet by 1980.

Initial A-10 Base Deployments

Unit Number	Location	Date activated	Tail Code
355th TFW	Davis-Monthan AFB, Tucson, Arizona	March 1976	DM
57th WTC	Nellis AFB, Nevada	October 1977	WA
354th TFW	Myrtle Beach AFB, South Carolina	October 1977	MB
81st TFW	RAF Bentwaters, United Kingdom	January 1979	WR
103rd TFG (ANG)	Bradley Field, Windsor Locks, Connecticut	May 1979	CT
174th TFW (ANG)	Hancock Field, Syracuse, New York	June 1979	NY
104th TFG (ANG)	Barnes Field, Westfield, Massachusetts	July 1979	MA
23rd TFW	England AFB, Alexandria, Louisiana	September 1980	EL
175th TFG (ANG)	Martin AFB, Baltimore, Maryland	355th TFW	355th TFW
917th TFG (AFRES)	Barksdale, Louisiana	October 1980	BD
926th TFG (AFRES)	New Orleans, Louisiana	January 1982	NO

This A-10 aircraft at RAF Bentwaters is in a metal hangar at a forward air base located in Germany. The 30 mm shell loader is located on the right. *Fairchild Republic archives via CAM*

A-10 aircraft, tail number 77-0192, is taking off from RAF Bentwaters or RAF Woodbridge in the United Kingdom. This base was close to Germany to allow for several forward deployments. *Fairchild Republic archives via LIRAHS*

An early A-10 aircraft from the 355th TFW, based at Davis-Monthan AFB, in 1976, which was the first operational A-10 base. The aircraft has the gray-and-white asymmetrical paint scheme that was used at that time. The use of gray was meant to help camouflage the A-10 against a pale sky. *USAF*

A quartet of A-10s assigned to the 355th TFW are flying over the mountains of southern Arizona. A few of these aircraft do not have the DM tail code painted yet. Davis-Monthan continues to be a major A-10 base to this day. *USAF*

A-10 is painted in the special mottle scheme for the Joint Attack Weapon Systems (JAWS) exercises that were held in November 1977 at Ft. Hunter Ligget, California. During these exercises, the A-10 worked with US Army AH-1 Cobra helicopters to improve on overall effectivity in attacking targets. *Fairchild Republic archives via LIRAHS*

A single A-10 aircraft is flying over ground targets during the JAWS exercises in November 1977. It can be seen that the special paint scheme allows the A-10 to blend in with the surrounding landscape. *Fairchild Republic archives via LIRAHS*

The first A-10 crash occurred at the Paris Air Show in June 1977. There was a low cloud ceiling, and the A-10, tail number 75-0294, came out of a loop that was too low, and the tail of the aircraft hit the ground. The aircraft crashed with the pilot still trapped in the cockpit section. *Fairchild Republic archives*

After impact, the fuel causes the aircraft to burst into flames. The pilot, Sam Nelson, was retrieved from the cockpit but died on the way to the hospital. The crash was ruled by the French investigating team to be pilot error as a result of the aircraft being flown too close to the ground when coming out of the loop. *Fairchild Republic archives*

By 1980, a new paint scheme was developed for the A-10 to match the European environment that the aircraft was to fly in. This scheme was designated as European I and consisted of three colors: medium green, olive green, and gunship gray. Although this scheme was retired by 1995, many museum display aircraft remain in this paint scheme, such as this one at Empire Science Aerospace Museum in Scotia, New York. *Ken Neubeck*

A single A-10 aircraft in the new European I paint scheme flies over trees during exercises in 1980. As can be seen, the special paint scheme allows the A-10 to blend in with the surrounding landscape. *Fairchild Republic archives via LIRAHS*

A-10 aircraft from the 355th TFW from Davis-Monthan are in the European I lizard paint scheme during exercises in the early 1980s in Arizona. This base remains very active to the present with A-10 aircraft that are regularly deployed to the Middle East or Afghanistan. *Fairchild Republic archives via LIRAHS*

This is one of the earliest examples of nose art from the early 1980s on the A-10, shown on this aircraft from Barksdale, Louisiana, where this A-10 flew with the 917th Fighter Group of the Air Force Reserves. The artwork features a warthog caricature over the nose section. *Fairchild Republic archives via LIRAHS*

An early-production A-10 from Davis-Monthan is undergoing aerial refueling from a KC-10A tanker aircraft. Aerial refueling is a critical operation for the A-10, and some long-duration missions in combat zones may require several refueling operations. *Fairchild Republic archives via LIRAHS*

This family photo of Republic-manufactured aircraft was taken in early 1985 and shows the A-10 on the right, an ANG F-105 Thunderchief located in front of it, and the last Republic aircraft, the T-46A, in front of that. *Fairchild Republic archives via CAM*

A tremendous amount of gun gas is generated during the firing of the 30 mm cannon, as seen on this A-10 based out of Alaska. The problem was recognized during early development, and as production began to ramp up in the 1980s, there were more events that were caused by gun gas ingestion into the engines, which would cause them to flame out. A joint USAF and Fairchild Republic tiger team was formed to investigate the problem and develop corrective action for this problem and other related engine flameout issues. *USAF photo by Airman 1st Class Jonathan Snyder*

By 1980, as more A-10s came into in service, it was observed that gun gas ingestion was a problem that caused the engine to flame out. One proposed fix was to add a deflector device onto the front of the cannon. *Fairchild Republic archives via CAM*

Associated with the baffle deflector device was the addition of louvers to front panels on the forward fuselage. *Fairchild Republic archives via CAM*

Another proposed fix for the problem was the extension of the nose on the aircraft, along with a new deflector door that opened when the gun was fired. All proposed structural fixes would result in vibration problems that resulted in cracks in the forward structure of the aircraft. The final fix was to have continuous ignition applied during gunfire, which is still implemented to the present day. *Fairchild Republic archives via CAM*

This aircraft is from the 354th TFW, based out of Myrtle Beach, South Carolina. This base was activated with A-10 aircraft in 1977. *Ken Kubik*

A-10 aircraft from the 23rd TFW, based out of England AFB, Louisiana, features the nose markings of the Flying Tigers. *Ken Kubik*

This 104th TFG ANG A-10 is based out of Westfield, Massachusetts, and displays the outline of the state on the nose. A-10s were reassigned from this base in 2005 due to base realignment.
Ken Kubik

This 175th TFG ANG A-10 is based out Martin AFB, Maryland, and the unit markings are displayed on the fabric engine covers. This is one of the longest-operating A-10 bases; it is still active to this date, with over thirty years of service.
Ken Kubik

These A-10 tail code markings are from different A-10 bases, circa 1990. The top row shows the tail codes for the 23rd TFW (EL) from England AFB, Louisiana, and the 103rd TFG (CT) from Bradley AFB, Connecticut. The bottom row shows the 354th TFW (MB) from Myrtle Beach AFB, South Carolina, and the 104th TFG (MA) from Westfield AFB, Massachusetts. All four of these bases were closed by the new century due to base realignment.
First three photos Ken Kubik, last photo Ken Neubeck

The A-10 Thunderbolt II is in the background of this photo, behind the nose section of its namesake, the P-47 Thunderbolt, the famed Republic Aviation aircraft from World War II. *Fairchild Republic archives via LIRAHS*

CHAPTER 5
Night / Adverse Weather Two-Seat A-10

After A-10 field deployment, it would become clear that the A-10 Warthog was configured as a daytime attack aircraft that would greatly depend on the pilot being able to visually spot targets on the ground. It also became clear that Warsaw Pact countries were conducting much of their training at night. The only way that the current version of the A-10 could operate at night was to use illumination flares, which would not be effective during nights of reduced visibility. Thus, a version of the A-10 that could fly at night and during adverse weather was needed.

The original 1972 Air Force A-10 System Specification stated, "the vehicle design shall allow for ease of growth to a two-place version for training (with combat capability), night / adverse weather attack." This effort would finally come to fruition when the DOD provided funding for the development of a night/adverse-weather (N/AW) prototype. This effort was jointly funded by the DOD and Fairchild Republic.

Fairchild leased the first DT&E aircraft (tail number 73-1664) from the Air Force for modification into an expanded N/AW two-seat aircraft. Modification of this aircraft into the two-seat prototype began in April 1978 at the Fairchild Republic Farmingdale plant, and it took over thirteen months to be completed. The N/AW A-10 had the addition of a second cockpit station, which would be occupied by the weapons system officer (WSO). The extra station would include a full duplication of the forward cockpit instruments except for the Heads-Up Display (HUD).

To accommodate the second pilot station, some of the existing airframe structure had to be removed in the area behind the cockpit. There was some strengthening of existing decking that was above the ammunition drum, in order to put in a floor for the second station. The existing titanium bathtub for the single-seat model would not be modified to protect the rear cockpit crew member; instead, a multilayer skin sandwich configuration would be used.

External changes to the airframe included the lengthening of the tail fin height, initially by 20 inches, in order to offset the aerodynamic changes caused by the front fuselage change, but after flight testing, it was determined that an increase of 6 inches was sufficient. The canopy design was changed from a single-piece clamshell canopy hinged at the rear of the cockpit to two individual canopy sections that opened sideways. While the pilot could still use the integral aircraft pull-out ladder, the WSO had to use a rollup ladder to board the rear cockpit.

New avionics were added to help in the N/AW mission. A forward-looking infrared radar (FLIR) was added to give expanded tracking function where it presented a realistic image of the terrain that appeared on the HUD. It could be used for target identification for the 30 mm gun, for INS updating, and as a secondary terrain avoidance monitor to the Westinghouse WX-50 multimode radar. The WX-50 radar would have modes for target indication, ground mapping, and terrain tracking and was able to target signals from surface-to-air missile batteries or antiaircraft guns.

A new INS made by Litton was installed on the aircraft. This included two Honeywell radar altimeters mounted in the tailplane, which would give continuous readouts of the height of the aircraft above ground, regardless of the aircraft's attitude. The FLIR, laser ranger, and terrain-following radar were placed in external pods that hung from various points under the aircraft.

The aircraft was assembled in Farmingdale and was delivered cross-country to Edwards AFB by cargo plane to begin flight testing by Fairchild Republic test pilots. The N/AW A-10 evaluator first flew on May 4, 1979. Flight testing included tactical evaluations of the detection of low-altitude flying targets, and gun attacks were introduced. Gunnery trials began on May 23, with the aircraft first performing a simulated daylight visual attack.

It became hard to simulate adverse weather conditions because of the clear climate at Edwards, so the HUD was covered and the canopy glass was coated to reduce visibility during a gunnery attack that was conducted using the FLIR. Night flights were initiated on May 29, and the new equipment for nighttime flying was checked out in the same manner as the reduced-visibility tests, except that no coating had to be applied to the HUD.

The evaluator was 2,000 pounds heavier than a regular A-10, which was the result of additional equipment and structural changes. The extra weight of the aircraft meant that the aircraft would require an additional 300 feet of runway for takeoff and about 80 more feet for landing in comparison to the single-seat A-10. There was also a reduction of 3 knots off the top speed of the aircraft when compared to the single-seat model. The evaluator accrued 120 hours of flight time over sixty-five flights during the five months of testing at Edwards by company test pilots before the aircraft was formally turned over to the Air Force in October 1979.

Flight testing of the plane by the Air Force began on October 23, and the official name of the flight program was the Air Force Preliminary Flight Evaluation (AFPE). This portion of the flight test program ended on December 4, with a total of forty-nine hours accrued over twenty-eight flights, with one-third of the flights taking place at night.

As would be expected for an aircraft with two crew members, there were well-defined duties and responsibilities for the two N/AW crew members, both in flying the aircraft and in attacking ground targets. Typically, during low-altitude flight it is the pilot who is responsible for flying the aircraft to the target while avoiding the ground. This is done by using the cockpit displays as well as using visual skills. In the meantime, the WSO in the back seat handles navigation by using the INS and radar ground mapping. The WSO also monitors the radar-homing and warning-system displays. Preliminary results were encouraging, since the evaluator's systems proved to be reliable in their performance and the crew members were able to handle operation of the new equipment.

Cost estimates at the time for converting an A-10 to a two-seater N/AW aircraft were $500,000 for the basic structural work and another $1 million for the additional equipment used in the N/AW functions. However, after the test period and despite the good reviews, the Air Force felt that the test results showed that one pilot could handle the additional workload of N/AW evaluator tasks. Indeed, a single-seat A-10 with enhanced capabilities such as Low Altitude Night Time Infrared Navigation (LANTIRN) was developed.

Before the end of A-10 production, there was an effort to obtain funding for a two-seat trainer version, after the Air Force asked for trade studies on this version. This two-seat trainer version, designated as the A-10B, was different from the N/AW evaluation in that the second seat would be added strictly for training purposes only, and there would be no advanced avionics for night flying that would be added. A proposal was made that twenty A-10B aircraft be tacked on to the original order of 713 aircraft, along with an option to retrofit existing A-10A models.

However, when Congress reviewed this proposal in 1983, the A-10B trainer idea faced stiff opposition in the Senate, and the requested A-10B aircraft were cut from the budget. Both high-level Air Force officers and congressmen felt that the plane was already simple enough to fly and that the current practice of training students to fly solo with the instructor in another aircraft was sufficient training.

In five years a minor variation of the A-10 would be developed: the OA-10A forward observer model. This aircraft would still have the 30 mm cannon, but in lieu of ordnance under the wing, the aircraft would have rocket launchers for firing white phosphorus rockets for marking potential ground targets for other aircraft and A-10s.

The N/AW evaluator would remain at Edwards AFB, and after 1979 the aircraft would eventually be stripped of its engines and avionics and become one of the aircraft exhibits displayed at the base. There was no follow-on or modification-type work for Fairchild Republic on the A-10 after the N/AW evaluator program. With the denial of funds for the proposed two-seat A-10B trainer, it effectively ended any hopes for extending the A-10 production program past 1984.

A-10 DT&E aircraft number 1 (tail number 73-1664) was modified at Fairchild Republic facilities in Farmingdale in 1979. *Fairchild Republic archives*

The N/AW two-seat A-10 evaluator aircraft undergoing flight testing at Edwards AFB during the summer of 1979. The canopy design was different from the single-seat A-10 model, since there were two separate side-opening canopies for the front and rear crew station positions. *Fairchild Republic archives via LIRAHS*

The evaluator had a number of access doors that were opened for the addition of new equipment. A small owl emblem is painted on the left side of the nose. Note that the pilot-boarding ladder is extended. For the rear station crew member, a rollup ladder was required for boarding. *Fairchild Republic archives via CAM*

The N/AW A-10 evaluator is inside a hangar at Edwards AFB during the spring of 1979. The N/AW evaluator had an owl theme, with owl's eyes painted on the engine covers. *Fairchild Republic archives via CAM*

The N/AW evaluator is coming in for a landing on the Edwards AFB runway with wing flaps fully extended during Air Force flight testing in October 1979. The additional weight of the evaluator over the single-seat A-10 aircraft required that an additional 80 feet was needed during the landing roll. The wings and flight controls were not modified on the evaluator. The Air Force would test the aircraft for almost three months. *Fairchild Republic archives via CAM*

Fairchild Republic Company test pilots prepare for a night mission in the N/AW evaluator and are awaiting instructions from the ground controller. The large pod assembly that is located underneath the center fuselage is the combination radar altimeter, FLIR, and laser pod. The aircraft is still painted in the original basic gray color that it had as a DT&E aircraft. It was not modified to the European I paint scheme that was present on A-10 aircraft at the time. *Fairchild Republic archives via CAM*

FWD FUSELAGE STRUCTURE BEFORE REWORK

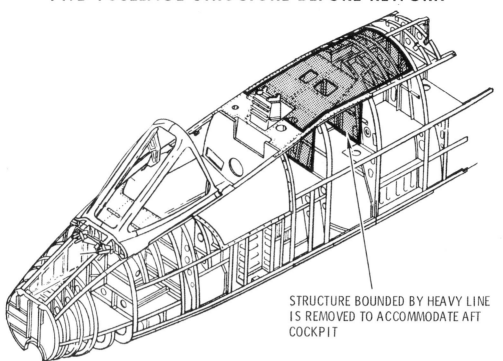

STRUCTURE BOUNDED BY HEAVY LINE
IS REMOVED TO ACCOMMODATE AFT
COCKPIT

FWD FUSELAGE STRUCTURE AFTER REWORK

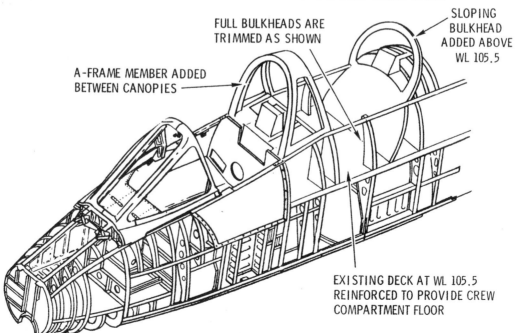

FULL BULKHEADS ARE
TRIMMED AS SHOWN

SLOPING
BULKHEAD
ADDED ABOVE
WL 105.5

A-FRAME MEMBER ADDED
BETWEEN CANOPIES

EXISTING DECK AT WL 105.5
REINFORCED TO PROVIDE CREW
COMPARTMENT FLOOR

There were some changes made to the forward station of the N/AW A-10. This included the modified Heads-Up Display (HUD) located on top of the console, along with an expanded TV monitor located on the top right of the console. Both of these were modified to accommodate the forward-looking infrared radar (FLIR) display. *Fairchild Republic archives*

The aft station would have all the flight controls that the forward station would have, with some additional equipment added. This includes a new Pave Tack virtual image display, which is located on top of the console, along with a new display located in the center of the console for the radar altimeter. A control panel for the WX-50 radar is located directly behind the control stick. *Fairchild Republic archives*

The N/AW evaluator is in flight over the California desert near Edwards AFB, with only the pilot in the front seat position, who conducting flight-handling tests over the California desert during the summer of 1979. The evaluator would be tested for over a seven-month period in 1979. *Fairchild Republic archives via CAM*

After the evaluation program ended, the N/AW A-10 evaluator would remain at Edwards AFB in the base museum. The engines and avionics have been stripped from the aircraft. *Dennis R. Jenkins*

CHAPTER 6
A-10 Production Ends

From the time that the A-10 entered into field service in 1975, it was never treated in the same class as the more glamorous speedy fighter jets that were favored by the US Air Force, such as the F-15 and F-16. The aircraft was slower than the fighters, and the close-air-support (CAS) mission in support of the Army was not considered as a primary Air Force fighter mission. Air superiority was considered the primary mission for the USAF, while ground support, though important, did not get the same attention.

Many experts thought that the US Army would have been a better fit as the primary operator, instead of the Air Force. There were informal suggestions from time to time about using the Army as the primary operator, along with Congress examining the CAS mission and who was best to fly it, but inevitably it would remain with the Air Force.

The A-10 was not an easy aircraft for the marketing department of Fairchild Republic to sell to foreign customers. It had to compete with foreign sales of the F-16 aircraft, which was the first choice for many countries because it was priced favorably.

Another stumbling block was that the 30 mm ammunition used in the A-10's gun consisted of spent uranium in the tip of the shell, allowing for maximum armor penetration. This material was initially restricted by the US government for export overseas, making it harder to sell the aircraft there.

At one point around 1982, there was interest from four different countries in purchasing A-10s: Indonesia, Japan, Morocco, and Thailand. The Fairchild marketing department produced a generic brochure on the A-10 and would tailor it to the potential threats in the geographic area for each country. The brochure for Morocco discussed the potential armored and infantry threats from its neighboring counties of Libya and Mauritania and stated that the A-10 is "uniquely suitable for [the] Moroccan environment."

There was moderate interest by Morocco and Thailand, but by 1983, nothing further had ensued. This was a critical date because the last A-10 production aircraft was being delivered to the Air Force in 1984, and it was hoped that foreign sales would have extended the production line.

The original quantity of 733 A-10 aircraft to be built was trimmed by Congress to a total of 713 aircraft. The last delivery was made in 1984, with a special ceremony held at the Hagerstown facility noting the final A-10 aircraft acceptance by the Air Force. There would be no additional aircraft to extend the production line, whether it be foreign sales or the A-10B trainer.

Prior to the end of the A-10 production program in 1984, Fairchild entered in a bidding competition on the next-generation trainer (NGT) proposal by the Air Force, and it would be the fallout of this program that led to the end of the company.

Fairchild emerged as the winner of the NGT proposal in late 1984, beating out Cessna and Rockwell. The NGT was designated as the T-46A aircraft, and there was also potential for the company to develop an attack version of this aircraft for foreign sales. However, in winning this fixed-price contract, which entailed building two preproduction aircraft and an initial production lot of ten aircraft, the company had cut pricing to the bone in order to win the contract, and the resulting financial issues caused the program to start off poorly.

Things came to a head in February 1985, when the official Air Force rollout ceremony of the first prototype T-46A aircraft took place in Farmingdale, but it was later discovered by the Air Force that the aircraft was missing several parts. This led to a series of Contractor Operation Reviews (COR) of Fairchild Republic in June 1985. The company failed the review, which led to the suspension of monthly progress payments. A reorganization took place in the company, and some improvement resulted;

however, political pressure from members in Congress now came into play, calling for the termination of the T-46A program.

Late in 1985, the parent company, Fairchild Industries, expressed a wish to exit the program unless the terms of the contract could be renegotiated. The company had already invested an additional $100 million of its own money into the program.

Despite the efforts of many, the end would come on Friday, March 13, 1987, when the Air Force reached a termination agreement for the T-46A program with Fairchild Industries, resulting in 500 employees losing their jobs on that day. By the end of 1987, the entire plant was shut down.

In September 1987, Grumman announced an agreement with the Fairchild Republic Company to acquire the A-10 program, along with the purchase of electronic equipment used in the program; in addition, Grumman agreed to take on 116 Fairchild Republic engineers who had worked on the A-10 program. Future upgrades for the A-10 would be handled for a time by Grumman, using the core of A-10 engineers who transferred from Fairchild.

In 1988, the Air Force began making a push for the F-16 to take over the CAS mission from the A-10. This involved some modification to the F-16, to make it an A-16 designation. The 174th Fighter Wing (FW) of the Air National Guard at Hancock AFB in Syracuse, New York, had changed over to F-16 aircraft from A-10 and were conducting tests with the F-16 in the ground support role. Arguments were made that with the increased speed of the F-16 over the A-10, it would be less of a target to enemy ground forces, although it was more vulnerable to ground fire.

Modifications to the F-16 aircraft for the CAS mission that were made in Syracuse included adding a mounted General Electric Pave Claw GPU-5/A 30 mm gun pod on the F-16 centerline strongpoint. The GPU-5/A was a much-smaller weapon than the GAU-8/A used on the A-10, since it had only four barrels and could be loaded with 353 rounds of 30 mm ammunition, which was much less than the A-10's drum capability of 1,350 rounds.

Things changed even further when the symbolic end of the Cold War came with the collapse of the Berlin Wall in November 1989. With this change, there was no need for keeping to the original levels of A-10, since there was now an effort toward reducing armored forces in eastern Europe. In addition, it was noted that some aspects of ground support were being handled by US Army helicopters, as evidenced by combat action in Grenada and Panama. The A-10 was now under scrutiny both by Congress and the Air Force for probable decommission. Some initial proposals toward scrapping large numbers of A-10 aircraft were being discussed by the end of 1989.

In late November 1989, Congress recommended that the Air Force be barred from spending fiscal year 1990 F-16 production funds until the Pentagon assured Congress that all alternatives would be tested for the F-16 performing the CAS mission. Additionally, the Pentagon was to report on CAS upgrades for the F-16 and the A-10 aircraft and also provide a report on whether responsibility for the fixed-wing CAS mission should be moved from the Air Force to the Army.

Both the Army and the Air Force opposed any changes to the existing responsibilities with regard to the CAS mission. General Colin Powell, the head of the Joints Chiefs of Staff, opposed any changes to the existing setup, noting, "It would sow considerable confusion and would be detrimental to the progress that had been made between the Army and the Air Force in recent years to resolve this issue." The Air Force debated whether to develop a new A-16 version or to modify existing F-16 aircraft for the CAS mission.

In late November 1990, the Air Force announced that it would retrofit existing F-16 aircraft for the CAS mission rather than procure a proposed A-16 version. It was stated as an affordability issue, since the Air Force would not be able to obtain funding both for a new A-16 and F-16 aircraft. The goal was to have the F-16 replace the A-10 in the inventory by 1990. After only fifteen years of service, it appeared that the A-10 would be headed toward the scrap heap to join the ashes of the closed Fairchild Republic Company.

A-10 Warthog from the 23rd TFW, based at England AFB, makes a rare stop at Republic Airport, located next to Fairchild Republic in the late 1980s, after the closure of Fairchild Republic. *Ken Kubik*

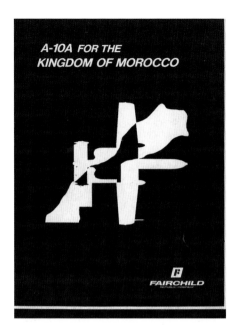

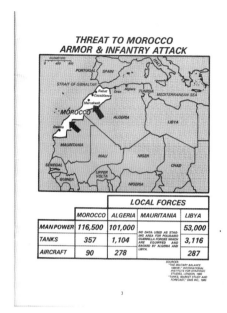

The A-10 was a difficult aircraft for Fairchild to market to foreign countries, for several reasons. First, there were initially restrictions by the US government on the export of spent uranium, which was used in the 30 mm cannon shells. In addition, the primary tank threat for the A-10 to counteract was in Europe, and aircraft were already deployed there by the US Air Force. Fairchild Republic's marketing department developed brochures for several different countries, such as shown above. For each brochure, the potential threat for that nation was described inside the brochure (such as the one shown for Morocco in top right photo). No foreign sales were ever made when the company was open, nor did the USAF sell any. *Fairchild Republic archives*

The fuselage section for the last A-10, tail number 82-0665, or aircraft number 713 off the production line, is seen here with Fairchild Republic shop crew and supervisors during early 1984. The wings for the aircraft are located in the tooling behind the fuselage in the background. *Fairchild Republic Archives via CAM*

One of the T-46 preproduction aircraft is in final assembly in the main building of Fairchild Republic in 1985. The last A-10 aircraft rolled down the same area only a year before. *Fairchild Republic archives via CAM*

The Syracuse ANG had originally flown A-10 aircraft in the early 1980s, but these were converted to F-16s such as this aircraft with the unit's marking shown here. During Operation Desert Storm in 1991, the unit was deployed to the region and was outfitted with the GBU-5/A gun pod, which would be mounted to the lower fuselage centerline. As subsequent actions would show, the pod was used only for one day because of issues of vibration and accuracy. At this point in the war, the A-10 would be the primary user of 30 mm ammunition that was directed at ground targets. *Ken Neubeck*

To make the F-16 capable of replacing the A-10 and more suitable for ground support, studies were conducted in which the GBU-5/A gun pod was added to the F-16 aircraft. The pod carried 353 rounds of 30 mm ammunition and could fire at a rate of 2,400 rounds per minute. A fully loaded pod adds about 2,000 pounds of weight to the aircraft. *USAF*

CHAPTER 7
A-10 at War: Operation Desert Storm

The A-10's primary mission was originally set up to be a tank killer in Europe to deal with the large number of tanks and artillery of Eastern Bloc nations. With that threat diminished by 1990 with the end of the Cold War, it was ironic that the next hotspot would be the Middle East.

Tensions had been building up between two Middle East border countries, Iraq and Kuwait, over the disputed Rumaila oil field, located at the border of the two countries. The situation reached a breaking point when Iraq's leader, Saddam Hussein, invaded Kuwait on August 2, 1990, with forces using the six-lane highway that connected Basra in Iraq to Kuwait City to invade.

At the time, Iraq's army consisted of over 4,000 tanks, including over 3,500 Soviet-made models: T-55, T-62, and the newer T-72, along with some older models such as the T-59 and T-69 that were originally supplied by China. In addition, Iraq had over 5,000 artillery pieces, including both self-propelled guns and cannons that were transported by trailers. Another major weapon in Iraq's arsenal was the Scud-B missile. This design was derived from the V-2 missiles that were used by the Germans at the end of World War II, with a range of 175 to 300 miles. It could carry either conventional explosive or chemical warheads and could be launched either by fixed launchers or mobile eighteen-wheel-truck launchers.

With the invasion of Kuwait by Iraq, Operation Desert Shield was ordered by President George W. Bush. The US would commit over 100,000 troops, along with hundreds of airplanes and tanks. With the buildup of forces over the next few months, the eventual plan was for the liberation of Kuwait. This would be the first major engagement of US armed forces to be deployed in significant numbers on foreign soil since Vietnam.

The US central command would be headed by Gen. H. Norman Schwarzkopf Jr. of the US Army, who was aware of the capabilities of the A-10 Warthog. There may have been some hesitation by the Central Command Air Force, under Lt. Gen. Charles Horner, to send A-10 aircraft to be deployed to Saudi Arabia. Whether this hesitation in deploying the A-10 was in fact true or not, Gen. Schwarzkopf, as head commander and an Army man, made his wish known to have A-10 aircraft deployed to the region against Iraqi tank forces.

On August 8, three A-10 squadrons—two from the 354th TFW from Myrtle Beach, and one from the 23rd TFW from England AFB, consisting of seventy-two aircraft—were deployed to Saudi Arabia. By the middle of August, this number was supplemented by an additional squadron from the 23rd TFW. These aircraft would make the transatlantic trip to Saudi Arabia and be based at King Fahd International Airport.

The original deployment of A-10s was complemented by additional aircraft from the 10th TFW from the United Kingdom, the 926th TFW from the New Orleans Naval Air Station in Louisiana, and the 602nd Tactical Air Control Wing (TACW) OA-10 group from Davis-Monthan AFB in Arizona. The total number of A-10s assigned to Saudi Arabia was initially 144 aircraft; however, eventual replacement aircraft would be required during the deployment, bringing the total to 152 aircraft.

TFW	TFS	Base Location	Aircraft
354th	353rd	Myrtle Beach AFB, South Carolina	26
354th	355th	Myrtle Beach AFB, South Carolina	24
23rd	74th	England AFB, Louisiana	24
23rd	76th	England AFB, Louisiana	27
906th	706th	Barksdale AFB, Louisiana	18
10th	511th	Alcony, United Kingdom	18
602nd	23rd	Davis-Monthan, Arizona	15

The A-10s deployed to Saudi Arabia were still in their European or lizard-style paint scheme, and the darker hues of green and brown seemed very much out of place in the light-brown landscape of the desert environment. No A-10 was repainted to any desert camouflage scheme similar to other US military equipment sent there.

The war started on the evening of January 16, 1991, and on that night, Capt. Tony Mattox of the 74th TFS flew the first A-10 combat mission in the aircraft's history, successfully destroying several Iraqi targets in Kuwait. At that point, Operation Desert Shield became Operation Desert Storm.

The war presented the A-10 Warthog with several new opportunities to perform missions that were not previously planned. Initially, the aircraft was to be deployed against conventional targets such as artillery, but it would soon be deployed in some unique missions that demonstrated its versatility. One new mission was Scud hunting.

When a Scud missile exploded in Israel on January 17, there was much concern that Israel would retaliate, possibly causing friction with the Arab countries that were part of the allied coalition. The Patriot missile defense system was provided to defend against these attacks, but there was a need for an aircraft that had the capability of loitering for hours to search out the Scud missile launch sites.

Out of this need came the role for the A-10 to be the key aircraft for searching out Scud sites throughout western Iraq. It could fly close to the ground and loiter over Iraqi territory for several hours on end, while waiting for signals from overhead surveillance aircraft with regard to newly targeted missile launcher sites. The A-10 would then trace the path back to the area where the missile was fired and then use its crew's visual skills to find the launcher. A-10s claimed the destruction of fifty Scud launchers during the war, although it is probable that some were decoy vehicles.

The extreme importance of the A-10 and its pilots in being able to take on the Scud search-and-destroy mission cannot be overstated. By having the A-10 perform this role, it freed up the rest of the coalition aircraft to be used in the main air campaign in Kuwait and Iraq. This was a major relief to the Air Force commanders, particularly because of the political sensitivity of any Iraqi Scuds landing in Israel and possibly drawing Israel into the conflict.

It was shortly after a successful A-10 Scud search-and-destroy mission that was conducted a few days after the war started that Gen. Horner made one of the famous statements about the A-10 during the war, at one of his staff briefings. This was reported immediately in the official base publication and would later be reported by *Washington Post* columnist Jack Anderson in his article "The Hero That Almost Missed the War." Horner would say, "I take back all the bad things I have ever said about the A-10. I love them. They're saving our asses!"

The A-10's loiter capability would be a key reason for another mission that the aircraft became involved with, which was the rescue of downed pilots over enemy territory. This mission would be nicknamed "Sandy" by the pilots, and the first such mission for the A-10 took place on January 21.

Two A-10 aircraft were deployed at 0800 that day as part of a search-and-rescue effort for a downed Navy aviator who had ejected from his F-14 aircraft, about 50 miles deep into the southern part of Iraq. The two A-10 pilots were Capt. Paul Johnson and Capt. Randy Goff, who during the course of this mission would refuel in the air four times.

When the A-10 pilots reached the Iraq-Saudi border, they communicated with the downed aviator, Lt. Devon Jones, through his emergency radio, and they tried to get a fix on his exact location. Both Jones and his back-seat aviator had ejected from their damaged F-14 during a low-altitude mission, and they landed miles apart, with one aviator captured by the Iraqis. Bad weather delayed the search, and it took four hours before the rescue pilots were able to determine where the aircraft was shot down and where Jones was located.

Once the rescue zone was established, the A-10s circled the area, providing security until the rescue helicopters arrived. The effort required over forty people and, at the time, was the deepest into enemy territory that a rescue had been made. While the A-10 pilots were loitering over the area, a large Iraqi pickup truck arrived and headed toward where Jones was. The A-10s attacked the truck with the 30 mm cannon, causing it to burst into flames. After the attack on the truck, the rescue helicopter came on the scene, and the Navy aviator was picked up and brought back to Saudi Arabia. The A-10 would be used for other rescue or Sandy patrols throughout the duration of the war.

The A-10 Warthog was effective in attacks both against artillery and other ground targets. From the outset of the war, the A-10 attacked fixed targets such as artillery pieces, airfields, bunkers, and military command posts. During the third day of the war, Iraqi artillery was shelling the northern Saudi oil refineries from their positions in Kuwait. A-10s were dispatched to attack these artillery positions to stop further attacks on the oil fields. Fixed artillery pieces, self-propelled guns, AA batteries, and FROG and SAM missile sites all were sitting ducks for the A-10 out in the open expanse of the desert; Warthogs attacked these targets by Maverick missiles or by gun.

A clever tactic was used by the A-10 Warthogs in attacks on artillery. The A-10s would fly over enemy territory at around 12,000 feet, which would draw fire from the Iraqi AA batteries, but the A-10 would be out of range for the AA guns. After these guns fired, the A-10 knew exactly where the guns were and would proceed to attack them either with Maverick missiles or the 30 mm cannon. The A-10 accounted for over 50 percent of Iraqi artillery pieces destroyed during the war.

February 6 was a pivotal day in the history of the A-10 Warthog. On that day, two different aspects of the aircraft were vividly demonstrated over central Kuwait. Capt. Bob Swain, a reservist flying for the 926th TFG, and a commercial aircraft pilot in civilian life, spotted an Iraqi helicopter, a Hind model. He tried to fire a Maverick missile at the target but could not lock on it, so he used his 30 mm gun in a head-on attack on the helicopter. On the first pass, he fired about seventy-five rounds at the target and then 200 rounds during the second pass, which brought the helicopter down. This was the first recorded air-to-air kill by an A-10 Warthog. On February 15, there was another air-to-air kill by A-10 pilot Capt. Todd Sheehy from the 511th TFW, on an Mi-8 helicopter.

Also on February 6, Capt. Paul Johnson (who had been involved with the rescue of the F-14 pilot a few weeks before) was flying his A-10, tail number 78-0664, during an attack on a SAM missile battery at about 7,500 feet, when the A-10 was hit by a SAM missile fired from the ground. The missile entered the underside of the right wing at the leading edge and caused damage resulting in a gaping hole of over 20 feet in diameter stretched across the wing, along with damage to the right main landing-gear housing. After the A-10 was hit, Johnson fought to regain control of the aircraft as it rolled about 120 degrees to the right, with the nose facing downward. He was getting ready to eject when after ten seconds, the aircraft responded and leveled off at 6,000 feet, which postponed the planned ejection. Johnson could fly at only 6,000 feet at a maximum of 190 knots, and his immediate concern was to get the aircraft across the border into Saudi Arabia so that he then could elect to eject. But after jettisoning remaining ordnance, he changed his mind when the aircraft picked up speed, and he decided to risk continuing to fly and landing the aircraft to the base at the King Fahd airport.

While still under fire, Capt. Johnson completed aerial refueling from a KC-10 tanker and was able to extend and lock the damaged right landing gear. He landed at King Fahd air base, even though the right tire shredded during the landing. After landing the aircraft, Johnson got out and kissed it. He was awarded the Air Force Cross for his courage in action, both for this mission and the previous rescue mission. Amazingly, this aircraft was repaired by the maintenance crew and returned to service in a few weeks!

Several combat events graphically demonstrated the survivability of the A-10. One was the well-publicized event of a 76th TFW aircraft (serial number 80-0168) flown by the wing commander, Col. David Sawyer, that had the tail section heavily damaged by an SA-16 SAM missile on February 15. Even though Col. Sawyer lost some of his pitch control due to the damage to the tail section, he was able to maintain overall control of his aircraft by flying straight and level at a set speed and was able to return back to base.

The primary role of tank killer supreme was the one that fit the A-10 the best. Although the USAF used other aircraft such as the F-111 and the F-16 in the role of attacking tanks, the A-10 was the one aircraft with the right speed and makeup to go after tank targets in an effective manner.

A-10s were especially effective in attacking convoys of tanks and military vehicles on the desert roads in Iraq and Kuwait. A-10 pilots would develop a trademark tactic during the war that began during the battle of Kahafji on January 29, when it destroyed thirty-five tanks and forty armored vehicles. When the A-10 made its first pass over an armored column, the aircraft would attack the first vehicle and the last vehicle of the column, effectively pinning all of the other vehicles in between. These sandwiched-in vehicles were left with little or no room to maneuver, and the A-10 Warthog would take a long turn prior to the next pass to allow the tank crew to leave their vehicles. Then the A-10 would swoop down for additional passes to take out the remaining vehicles.

One of the most memorable days occurred on February 25, just as the ground war started. Two A-10 pilots, Capt. Eric Salomonson and Lt. John Marks, flew as a two-aircraft tandem shortly after dawn and were dispatched to southern Iraq to search for Republican Guard tanks. Each plane lifted off the runway with a full complement of 30 mm rounds and a payload of Mavericks and cluster bombs. Low clouds and light rain required visual spotting, which entailed the pilots having to resort to looking for tank tracks in the sand and following them to revetments that the Iraqis dug up to protect their tanks. The pilots would follow the churned-up tracks of the tanks that resulted when these vehicles left the road to proceed to their new locations.

Once the tanks were spotted, one Warthog would roll in for the attack while the other Warthog would protect the attacking plane's rear. Each attacking plane used a combination of firing Maverick missiles and 30 mm shells from the cannon. By using this tactic, the pilots were able to destroy four T-72 tanks apiece during their first mission. After returning to base, they received the call to go to Kuwait to engage more tank targets. The two pilots would fly two more missions together that day over Kuwait, bringing the total time in the air to seven hours for each. At day's end, the total for the pair was twenty-three tank kills, with Salomonson getting eleven and Marks getting twelve. This reflected past history when Hans Rudel in his *Stuka* attacked Russian tanks on the eastern front in World War II.

While this particular event was well publicized in US newspapers, it is important to note that other A-10 Warthogs were recording the moving Iraqi tanks at the same time. The overall A-10 Warthog fleet was averaging an effective kill rate of over twenty-five tanks a day, and this along with the efforts of other aircraft was making a sizable dent in Iraq's armed forces.

The A-10 was able to fly around the clock and conduct effective night attack against Iraqi targets. The Iraqis were hiding many of their tanks and artillery pieces by using various means of camouflage,

as well as by partially burying some equipment. The Iraqis counted on the cloak of darkness at night to continue to hide their equipment; however, a clever improvisation on the A-10 would allow the aircraft to conduct night missions.

The 355th TFS from Myrtle Beach was chosen to be the so-called Night Hogs; these A-10s would fly in pairs, with one aircraft flying fully powered on, and the other aircraft powered with minimal cockpit instrumentation on as well as having the TV Maverick monitor on. The latter pilot would use his TV monitor to read infrared imaging through the seeker eye of the Maverick missile and would search for any bumps or irregularities on his screen, indicating infrared images in the desert sand that might contain a buried Iraqi tank. Metal in the sand cools more slowly at night than the surrounding sand and shows up as a hot target for the monitoring pilot. The other pilot would then launch a Maverick at the target, and a successful hit would be determined when explosions occurred (called "tank plinking").

Desert Storm was the debut of the OA-10 forward air control (FAC) version of the aircraft, which would be used in the important reconnaissance mission of target identification and marking. The OA-10 Warthogs differ from the A-10 Warthog only in the type of equipment that is carried on the wing pylons. Instead of a mix of bombs or Maverick missiles that the A-10 normally carries, the OA-10 carries phosphorus rocket launchers that are used to mark targets. Additionally, each OA-10 is equipped with two AIM-9 air-to-air missiles that are used for potential defensive situations against Iraqi aircraft. The OA-10 would still have a fully loaded 30 mm cannon that could be used for ground attacks when the opportunity arrived. A total of fifteen OA-10s from the 602nd Tactical Air Control (TAC) wing from the 23rd Tactical Air Support Squadron (TASS) from Davis-Monthan were deployed from King Fahd International Airport.

The FAC missions flown by the OA-10 pilots were at times dangerous, particularly when trying to mark targets while being attacked by AA fire from the ground and calling in other aircraft to attack these targets at the same time. This mission required a lot of pilot skills in reading maps, using binoculars and then firing the white phosphorus rockets at potential targets for other aircraft to attack. During Desert Storm, the OA-10 aircraft would mark or identify over 3,000 targets for other attack aircraft, and OA-10s would fire over 16,000 rounds of 30 mm shells.

As the war wound down, the Iraqi soldiers were abandoning many of their positions and leaving their tanks as well. One of the last major attacks on Iraqi armor took place on February 26, when the army was retreating on the six-lane Highway 80, which connected Kuwait City to Basra in Iraq. A combination of tanks, trucks, and stolen cars on the highway would be spotted by coalition surveillance aircraft, and US armed forces would dispatch A-6, A-10, F-16, and AH-64 helicopters to the highway to attack the retreating forces. The resulting carnage was nicknamed the "Highway of Death," and there would be similar attacks on retreating Iraqi forces on the coastal roads leaving Kuwait City as well.

Media coverage of this carnage led to the end of the war. A ceasefire took place on March 2, and within a few weeks, US forces would be coming back home, including many of the A-10 pilots and aircraft. The following table is the official USAF tally of the A-10s' kill total during the forty-two-day war:

Target	Number Destroyed
Tanks	987
Artillery pieces	926
APC	500
Trucks	1,106
Military structures	112
Radar installation	96
Bunkers	72
Scud missile launchers	51
AAA batteries	50
Command posts	28
FROG missiles	11
SAM missile sites	9
Fuel tanks	8
Aircraft (in air)	2
Aircraft (on ground)	12
Helicopter (in air)	2

US Army estimates are much higher than the confirmed kills, crediting the A-10 with between 25 and 50 percent of Iraq's 4,000 tanks, more than 50 percent of the 4,000 artillery pieces, and more than 30 percent of Iraqi armored personnel carriers.

The A-10 was the second most active aircraft in terms of the number of sorties flown and total number of USAF aircraft deployed, behind the F-16, which had 249 aircraft deployed and over 13,450 flying hours.

USAF statistics show that the A-10 flew an average of 2.2 hours per mission during the war, with over 19,000 flying hours accrued against 8,524 total sorties. The Warthog flew more than one mission per day per aircraft, and this was reflected in the mission-capable rate of 96 percent, which exceeded the Air Force average of 92 percent total for Desert Storm. The A-10 fleet averaged over 200 sorties and 400 flying hours per day. Just under a million 30 mm rounds were fired by A-10s, and 5,000 AGM65 Mavericks were fired. OA-10 aircraft fired almost 3,000 rockets for target marking.

Six A-10s were lost during the war, with five of them lost in action and another that was lost during a crash landing at base. Three A-10 pilots were killed, and three ejected from their damaged A-10s and became POWs. February 15 was the worst day for the A-10, with two from the 353rd TFS that were lost when conducting interdiction missions behind the Iraqi lines. It was at that point that the A-10 missions were refocused to frontline support.

In April 1991, a number of congressional hearings were conducted in order to assess the effectiveness of the weapon systems used during the war. One of the original designers of the A-10 and F-16 aircraft, Pierre Sprey, would testify that "initially the USAF and Gen. Horner resisted deploying any A-10s in support of Desert Shield," and that "it was a tribute to Gen. Horner's character and dedication to combat that he informed both his staff and higher headquarters that he was wrong about the A-10 and that it 'saved' his campaign." He would further state that the idea of replacing the A-10 with the F-16 is "one of the most monumentally fraudulent ideas that the Air Force has ever perpetrated."

Sprey noted that the A-10 was the real hero of the air war, even though it represented only one-twelfth of the fighter force, yet it flew over one-third of the sorties and accounted for two-thirds of the tank kills claimed, as well as 90 percent of the artillery kills. He noted that the A-10 was the only aircraft tough enough at surviving AA fire, while the F-111 and F-16 were too vulnerable to ground fire to be useful in the ground support role.

One immediate result after the war was the cessation of the F/A-16 effort. The F-16 aircraft from the 138th TFS, from the 174th ANG unit at Hancock AFB in Syracuse, New York, was deployed in Desert Storm with the 30 mm gun pod attachment, but after one day the use of the gun pod was discontinued because the gun would shake too much when firing and was not able to maintain either accuracy or penetration on Iraqi tanks.

The ensuing discussion and testimony would prove what would become an old adage involving the A-10: during wartime, the Air Force loved the aircraft, but during peacetime, they would disparage it.

This A-10 from the 23rd TFW Flying Tigers has the standard nose markings of that unit, with the shark's teeth and eyes applied to the forward nose section. The 23rd TFW provided the most A-10 aircraft during Operation Desert Storm, totaling fifty-one. This particular aircraft is preparing for a tank-killing sortie, since it is equipped with four Maverick missiles in addition to a full load for the 30 mm gun. The contrast between the A-10's European I paint scheme and the desert environment can be seen clearly here. *USAF photo by SSgt Robert V. Pease*

Once the coalition forces seized control of the air, there was no problem for the A-10 to fly unimpeded against ground targets, despite its dark colors against the desert sand background. *USAF photo by Tech. Sgt Rose Reynolds*

Crew from the 23rd TFW are loading up the A-10 with 30 mm ammunition, using an automatic loader. During Desert Storm, the A-10 fired over 960,000 rounds. *USAF photo by Sgt Prentes Tramble*

Operation Desert Storm brought out the World War II tradition of artwork applied to the nose of the A-10. This A-10 from the 706th TFW had kill markings in the form of a target symbol, and the tally mark next to it. *USAF*

A-10 aircraft from the 353rd TFS, out of Myrtle Beach AFB, tail number 78-677, was given the moniker "Kiss of Death." The aircraft destroyed a number of targets, including eight tanks. After the war, this aircraft would be retired to the Davis-Monthan "boneyard" in Arizona in 1992. *Anthony Abbott*

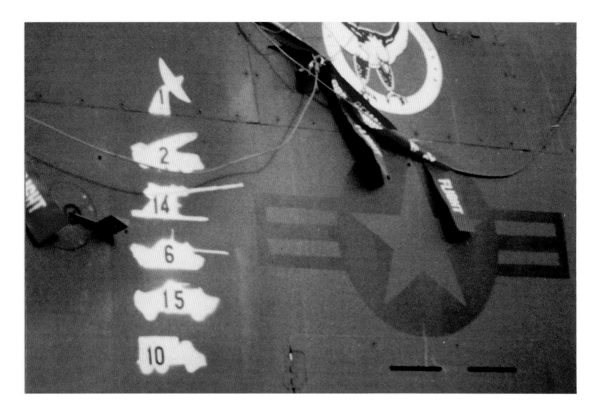

The kill markings for A-10, tail number 78-0665, from the 354th TFW were applied in the unique manner where the numbers of kills would be placed inside the target symbol. *Fred Schlenker III*

This A-10 aircraft from the 353rd TFS, out of Myrtle Beach AFB, tail number 78-677, had the moniker "Midnight Express." It was one of the A-10s that flew nighttime missions, and it was credited with eleven tank kills, including eight tanks. After the war, this aircraft would be retired to Davis-Monthan AFB, Arizona, in 1993. *Anthony Abbott*

This A-10 Warthog, tail number 80-0186, was flown by the 23rd TFW wing commander, Col. Sawyer, and it was able to return back to base despite severe damage to the tail section from impact from an SA-16 missile launched from the ground. *USAF*

This is a close-up view of the tail of Col. Sawyer's aircraft, showing extensive damage from the SAM missile. This aircraft was repaired and returned to service. It would be temporarily retired in 1998 to the AMARC facility at Davis-Monthan, returned to service in 1999, and then retired to be a display at the Evergreen Aviation and Space Museum in Oregon. *USAF*

One of the most publicized events involving the A-10 during Desert Storm was this A-10 (78-0664) flown by Capt. Paul Johnson that was hit by a SAM missile. Despite wing and engine damage, the A-10 flew back to base. *USAF*

Close-up photo of Capt. Johnson's aircraft shows that the leading edge of the right wing and the right-side main landing-gear pod are severely damaged. Repairs were performed on this aircraft, and it was returned to service in the war. *USAF*

A-10, tail number 77-0205, nicknamed "Chopper Popper," from the 906th TFG, has the Iraqi flag located on its left side, marking an air-to-air kill of an Iraqi helicopter. This was the first of two air-to-air kills by the A-10 in Operation Desert Storm. *Anthony Abbott*

The newest A-10 tail number to participate in Desert Storm was 82-0665, which was with the 23rd TFW.
This was the last A-10 off the production run and was appropriately nicknamed the "Last Tiger."
Anthony Abbott

This photo graphically shows one of the obstacles of locating Iraqi tanks. Tanks would often be partially buried in revetments, making it difficult for aircraft to locate them. The nighttime missions conducted by A-10 aircraft from the Myrtle Beach contingency to locate these tanks through the infrared eye of the Maverick missile would prove to be an effective means to locate and destroy them. *USAF*

A-10, tail number 79-0158, from the Myrtle Beach 355th TFS, is one of the several A-10 aircraft that participated in the nighttime search-and-destroy missions of tanks and other targets buried under the desert sand. *Fred Schlenker III*

A repair technician is applying a metal patch to cover bullet holes that were incurred from ground fire on an A-10A. Many A-10s had holes in the aircraft as the result of ground fire during the war. *USAF*

An engine mechanic is repairing an oil leak on the rear section of an A-10 engine that was damaged by ground fire. *Fred Schlenker III*

This destroyed Iraqi military convoy of tanks and trucks was probably attacked by A-10s that used the technique of attacking the lead and rear vehicles of the column in order to pin the other vehicles that are in between. *DOD photo by SSgt Dean Wagner*

This destroyed Iraqi T-55 tank bears the telltale sign of an A-10 attack, with a hole in the turret that was most likely made from a 30 mm shell fired by the A-10 gun. A-10 aircraft destroyed almost 1,000 Iraqi tanks during the war, constituting a quarter of the Iraqi army's tank force. *DOD*

A-10 pilot from the 23rd TFW is preparing for a mission during Desert Storm. A-10 pilot workload was very high during the forty-two-day war, in which overall, each A-10 aircraft averaged over one mission a day. *USAF photo by Sgt Prentes Tramble*

A-10, serial number 78-0686, with nose art; "Night Penetrator" was a member of the Falcons of the 355th TFS and was one of the Night Hogs that flew nighttime missions during the war. *Anthony Abbott*

Late on February 25, the Iraqi army began a mass retreat of military vehicles and stolen civilian vehicles from Kuwait on Highway 80. The movement was detected by allied forces and A-10s were dispatched. During the first wave of attack, the front and the rear of the column were attacked, pinning all vehicles in between. The aerial attack continued into the next day and was labeled as the "Road of Death." Media coverage of this event prompted a ceasefire and an end to the war. *DOD photo by Tech. Sgt. Joe Coleman*

A very rare shot of a large contingent of over 140 A-10 aircraft was taken from a hill overlooking the Kind Fahd airport after the war ended. This event was nicknamed "Elephant Walk" and was largest A-10 grouping ever. *USAF photo by SSgt. Robert V. Pease*

CHAPTER 8
New Life: Re-wing and A-10C Model

The A-10 Warthog's success during Operation Desert Storm gave it new recognition that would finally make it a major weapon system for the US Air Force. It became obvious that the aircraft was here to stay and that no other aircraft was going to take over the CAS role, whether it was a modified F-16 or a US Army helicopter.

Beginning in 1990, A-10s were modified to incorporate the Low Altitude Safety and Targeting Enhancements (LASTE) System, which provided computer-aided improvements to the aircraft such as a ground collision avoidance system (GCAS) to issue warnings of impending collision with the ground. There was also the inclusion of an enhanced attitude control (EAC) function for providing additional aircraft stabilization during gunfire, as well as a low-altitude autopilot system (LAAS), along with other targeting improvements made to the computer systems.

The results of these modifications were striking when the A-10 aircraft from the 175th TFW unit from Martin ANG took top honors during the Gunsmoke competition event that was held at Nellis AFB in October 1991. Additional improvements to the A-10 in the area of NVIS (night-vision imaging system) modification were made over the next decade.

At the end of Desert Storm, there were still over 650 A-10s in the USAF inventory, which were originally designed to counteract the large number of tanks owned by Warsaw Pact nations. In light of the changing global situation in 1992, with the Warsaw Pact dissolved and the target-rich environment of tanks going away, 650 A-10s were more than what would be needed for future conflicts, since there were fewer tank forces remaining in the world.

Therefore, some reduction in the A-10 fleet size was going to be needed. A plan had to be developed to carefully manage the fleet of A-10 Warthogs so that the aircraft would be able to continue in the inventory for many years to come, given that new aircraft was being developed for its missions, as well as the fact that its

original manufacturer, Fairchild Republic, was gone, and all tooling for spares parts was gone as well.

Earlier-production A-10s were approaching the end of their life, with 12,000 to 13,000 flight hours accrued, and would soon be retired. These A-10s would be spared the scrap heap, with many of them permanently stored at the AMARC facility located at Davis-Monthan AFB in Tucson, known as the boneyard, where they would be available to provide certain structural parts that could be used as spares for the remaining A-10s still in service. Some A-10s were retired and used as museum exhibits or gate guards at air bases throughout the United States. Additionally, there were a number of base closures and realignments as the result of the BRAC 1991 commission. A-10 bases such as Myrtle Beach and England AFBs were closed, and the A-10 aircraft that were there would be assigned to new locations

In 1993, in an effort to reduce the surplus of A-10s in the inventory, the US government proposed a sale of fifty A-10 aircraft to Turkey. There were additional rumors of other foreign countries in South America being interested in purchasing A-10 aircraft as well. However, the Turkish deal eventually fell through because of financial issues related to the support package. This would be the very last time that foreign military sales and the A-10 were mentioned together again.

There was consideration in 1993 of using retired military aircraft such as the A-10 to help both state and federal government in fighting forest fires in the western US states. This has now been going on for a number of years, with retired Navy aircraft such as the S2F Tracker and the P2V Neptune being converted to be able to carry large volumes of fire retardant and spreading it over a fire area.

In the case of the A-10, it had the ideal speed and maneuverability to tackle a fire, and a number of western fire services expressed an interest in taking a retired Warthog out of service and modifying it for firefighting. Some concepts that were developed resulted in a proposal known as Firehog Airtankers in 1993. The main modification featured the addition of a large underbelly under the aircraft that would hold the fire retardant.

The proposal eventually got as far as a demonstration of two A-10 aircraft in flight, arranged by the Watershed Fire Council of Southern California for firefighters in September 1997, with a final summary report being written that cited the flexibility of the A-10, particularly in the area of the speed brakes, which were employed to change speed quickly, a feature desired for firefighting. However, despite interest by civilian fire services, the Air Force did not formally release any retired A-10 to actually be modified.

With A-10 service being extended longer in the USAF, a number of aircraft upgrades were going to be needed, particularly if the aircraft was going to remain in service past the projected date of 2020 and beyond. The proposed upgrades were focused into two major areas: structural and electronics. Many of the upgrades commenced at the beginning of the twenty-first century.

In the area of structural upgrades, it was known that a number of the older A-10 aircraft tail numbers did not have the benefit of production improvements in the wing section that were made by Fairchild Republic in the later years of the production program to allow for longer wing life. Additionally, there were cracks that were found in the wing area of these older aircraft that would result in the temporary grounding of the fleet in 2008.

A wing-strengthening modification program designated as "Hog Up" took place at the AMARC facility located in Davis-Monthan AFB in Arizona, beginning in 2009. By modifying the wings of current aircraft, the A-10 is estimated to gain an additional 8,000 flying hours in service.

The wing-strengthening program was meant to be an interim fix for the A-10s currently in service. A larger contract of $2 billion was awarded to Boeing in 2007 for the A-10 wing replacement program, where Boeing would manufacture up to 242 enhanced-wing assemblies that would be retrofitted into the A-10 fleet in the future.

Besides the structural upgrades, the advent of advanced electronics and communication technology allowed for some significant upgrades to the A-10 to be made. Beginning in 1999, the A-10 was modified to have GPS system capabilities added to the aircraft, with an external GPS dome antenna added to the spine of the aircraft, behind the cockpit. This allowed the location of the aircraft to be tracked in the battlefield by AWAC aircraft. GPS upgrades for the A-10 were completed in 2003.

An improved communication system for line-of-sight communications was added to the aircraft in the form of the ARC-210 radio system, with a new antenna that was also located on the spine of the aircraft, behind the cockpit. Modifications for this system began in 2008. This system was an improvement over the existing type of communications used by the A-10, particularly in a mountainous and hilly environment, which can adversely affect reception and transmission of radio signals.

A number of A-10s received the AN/AAR-47 infrared missile-warning system beginning in 2008, which is a passive electro-optic missile-warning system that provides a warning of approaching surface-to-air missiles to the pilot in the cockpit. This system resulted in the addition of two sensors located in the tail cone section of the aircraft, along with forward sensors located on the tip of both wings.

The most significant change to the A-10 was the Precision Engagement (PE) program, in which A-10A models were converted to A-10C models. The change to the C model would include going from the current video display to two multifunction color displays located on the main cockpit panel, along with the addition of an up-front controller on the top of the main cockpit panel. The addition of the up-front controller allowed for better coordination of different systems by the pilot in one spot in the cockpit. Conversions to the C model began in 2007 and were performed at Hill AFB in Utah.

In the twenty-year period since the end of Desert Storm, the A-10 has been made to be an even more flexible and viable weapon system that is able to meet the demands of different locations around the world. With fewer tanks to be attacked, newer targets include concealed artillery or missiles posts that are nestled in remote mountain locations that conventional aircraft and helicopters are not able to attack.

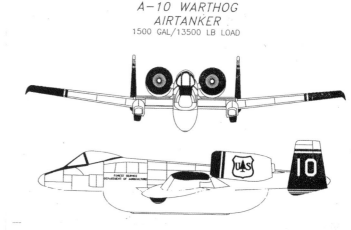

After Operation Desert Storm, the A-10 Warthog received a new lease on life, becoming a major fixture in the US Air Force. There were changes in A-10 base locations, such as the closing of England AFB in Louisiana, which had the 23rd TFW, a wing that was later transferred to Pope AFB and then to Moody AFB. There was also a return to the original gray paint scheme. *Ken Neubeck*

This is a preliminary drawing that came out in 1992 for what a modified A-10 would like for use in fighting forest fires. The modification featured the addition of a 1,500-gallon tank to the lower fuselage of the aircraft. The design never got into the next stage.

These A-10 Warthogs have protective covering around the forward fuselage and the engine nacelles. They are located in the desert at the AMARC facility or the "boneyard" at Davis-Monthan AFB, Tucson, Arizona. Some of these A-10s are getting their wings strengthened as part of "Hog Up," while other A-10s, who have reached the end of their operating life and are being used for spare parts to support the fleet, will be used as a supply source for spare parts to support remaining A-10s in service. *Ken Neubeck*

Technicians have just removed a wing section from the A-10 aircraft on the right, in a disassembly area in the desert sand of the AMARC facility. The wing section will be brought to a staging area and then into a plant where structural modifications are made. *USAF photo by Staff Sgt. Bennie J. Davis III*

Removed wing sections are in the staging area outside of the DMARC facility located in Davis Monthan in Tucson, Arizona, ready for structural modifications that will make the wings thicker and stronger. *Ken Neubeck*

Several A-10 aircraft in the hangar at Hill AFB are undergoing the conversion from the A to the C model. Most of the conversion work is focused primarily in the cockpit area of the aircraft, with some external antennas added through the aircraft fuselage. In addition to GPS being added, there is a precision engagement (PE) upgrade. Upgrades began in 2007, with groups of A-10 from different squadrons undergoing the upgrade at Hill AFB. The complete fleet of just over 360 A-10 aircraft was converted to the C model in approximately four years. *Bryan William Jones*

Technicians at Hill AFB, Utah, are in the process of modifying the cockpit of an A-10A aircraft into the A-10C model. Like in most aircraft, the A-10 cockpit has a significant amount of cables and wiring for the instruments. As part of the conversion effort, the forward canopy section has been propped up to allow complete access for the technicians to rework all the wire harnesses located behind the main cockpit panels for the instruments and gauges in the cockpit. Many cables are the original ones from the original production, and some will require replacement as well. *Bryan William Jones*

Beginning in 1999, the A-10A was modified to add GPS system capabilities to the aircraft. This included the addition of a dome antenna that is located on top of the fuselage, behind the canopy. GPS upgrades were completed in 2003. Beginning in 2008, an additional antenna was added to the top fuselage, behind the GPS dome antenna. This is for the beyond-the-line-of-sight airborne radio ARC-210 system, which was added to most A-10 aircraft in order to improve communications between the pilot and ground troops. This came from war experiences in Afghanistan, where the A-10 flew in and out of mountainous areas that disrupted radio transmissions. *Ken Neubeck*

Shortly after the A-10C upgrade was completed, there was the incorporation of the AN/AAR-47 infrared missile-warning system, which begin in 2008. The AN/AAR-47 is a passive electro-optic missile-warning-system design to provide warning of surface-to-air missiles (SAMS) and pass on the information to a display in the cockpit. This required the addition of sensors on the wing tips, as well as two cylinder-shaped sensors to the end of the tail section, as seen here. SAM missiles are a constant threat to the A-10 both in Afghanistan and Iraq. *Ken Neubeck*

The A-10C cockpit features a major upgrade from the original A-10A cockpit by going to a glass cockpit concept. All instruments have been upgraded to night vision instrument system (NVIS) technology, making the A-10 a more complete aircraft. *Ton Smolders*

The helmet for the pilot was updated with additional features to be used with A-10C aircraft. In addition, the control stick has been changed, using the F-16 aircraft version. The new stick has additional switches to handle more weapon functions. *Ton Smolders*

The upgrade of the A-10A to the A-10C version is the result of the Precision Engagement program that began in 2006. Several changes were made to the instrumentation of the A-10 console. Located on the top of the console is the new up-front controller (UPC), which allows the pilot the ability to switch between different modes without having to look down. Two multifunctional color displays (MFCDs) have been added to the top left and right corner of the console. Most of the flight instruments are the same as before, with the major change being that they are now NVIS compatible. *John Gourley*

Each multifunction color display (MFCD) consists of an LCD display that is surrounded by various function buttons. The MFCD can display a wide range of information, including weapons, navigation, and communications, making the A-10C a true glass cockpit design. Compared to the original monitor used in the A-10A, which could display video from only two weapon stations, the MFCD allows for navigation information to be displayed on one of the MFCDs, while the other MFCD can be used to set up ground targets. *John Gourley*

CHAPTER 9

Yugoslavian Wars: A-10s in the Balkans

It was not long after the end of Desert Storm that the A-10 would once again be deployed into combat and prove its value as a close-air-support aircraft. This time, action took place in eastern Europe in the region of the former Yugoslavia, not far from the original plan of anticipation of operation for the A-10 Warthog when it was first produced in the 1970s.

There were three separate NATO operations—Operation Deny Flight, which began in 1993 over Bosnia; Operation Deliberate Force, which took place over Bosnia in 1994; and Operation Allied Force, which took place over Kosovo in 1999.

As early as April 1993, a dozen OA-10s were deployed from the 81st Fighter Squadron (FS) from Spangdahlem, Germany, and were based in Aviano, Italy, to fly operations over disputed areas of Bosnia as part of Operation Deny Flight. As of 1994 the operation was designated as Operation Deny Force. In August 1994, A-10 aircraft attacked an M-18 tank destroyer operated by the Bosnian Serbs. OA-10s along with NATO aircraft participated in another attack on a Serbian tank a month later.

It would be the result of an attack by Bosnian Serbs in July 1995 on the Bosnian town of Srebrenica, in which over 8,000 civilians were killed, that large-scale NATO air strikes were authorized to deal with future acts of Serb aggression. After another attack that occurred on August 28, 1995, where Serb forces launched a mortar shell at the Sarajevo marketplace that killed thirty-seven people, NATO officially launched Operation Deliberate Force, with large-scale bombing of Serb targets in the region.

Because of the close air support that was required in supporting this operation, the A-10 was one of the USAF aircraft provided for the NATO effort. All told, during Operation Deliberate Force there were twelve A-10 aircraft that took part, operating out of the air base at Aviano, Italy. During this conflict, the A-10 fired

about 10,000 rounds of 30 mm ammunition, along with about two dozen Maverick missiles that were fired.

The bombing lasted until September 20, 1995, when hostilities ended. Altogether there were attacks on over 300 individual targets by NATO aircraft during Operation Deliberate Force.

The A-10 continued to fly in this region as part of the resumption of Operation Deny Flight activities until about 1997 as part of NATO surveillance in the region. Although hostilities had ended in Bosnia, the unrest in the region was still present, and war would again flare up in a region that was farther south from Bosnia, in the province of Kosovo in 1999. NATO formed Operation Allied Force with the purpose of stopping the Serbian army from conducting military operations against Albanians living in Kosovo.

As was the case in 1993, the Aviano air base in Italy was the site of the initial deployment of A-10 aircraft when six A-10 Warthogs from the 81st FS from Spangdahlem arrived in January 1999. By March, the 81st FS force in Aviano was expanded to fifteen A-10 aircraft. When the A-10 was moved to Gioia del Colle air base, located in southern Italy, later in March, the number increased to twenty-three aircraft. In May, an additional eighteen ANG A-10 aircraft from the 110th FW from Battle Creek, Michigan, were deployed to Trapani, Sicily, to bring the total amount of A-10 aircraft in Operation Allied Force to forty-one.

The air war began on March 24 by NATO, with attacks on Serbian targets in Kosovo and in Serbia. On April 7, the A-10 was used in combat in this region for the first time, when the aircraft was used to attack vehicle columns around Kosovo. Attacks on Serbian tanks and armored vehicles continued throughout April and into May when weather conditions permitted.

The A-10 was called to aid in downed-pilot rescue missions, or "Sandy," for which the A-10 provided air cover. The first such incident in Kosovo occurred on March 27, when two A-10s from the 81st FS provided support in the successful rescue of an F-117 pilot who ejected near Belgrade, Serbia. The A-10s required refueling from a KC-135 tanker during the mission, and because the rescue took place at midnight, flares were fired from the A-10s in order for the tanker to locate them. The second such rescue took place on May 1, when four A-10s lead an effort to rescue an F-16 pilot who was shot down in northern Serbia.

Weather played a major factor in the success of the attacks. Because of the reluctance to have aircraft fly low, most attacks were conducted higher than normal and with cloudy conditions present; this made it hard to attack targets. In addition, there were concerns about avoiding civilian casualties, which was made difficult by the proximity of military targets near civilian populations.

There were no A-10 aircraft that were lost during Operation Allied Force, although a few aircraft did receive damage from ground fire during the seventy-eight-day war. On May 2, an A-10 aircraft with tail number 81-0967, piloted by Maj. Phil "Goldie" Haun, had just completed a strafing run on Serbian tanks when it was hit by an SA-14 missile in the right engine, but Hawn was able to land his aircraft in friendly territory at an airfield in Skopje, Macedonia. The aircraft was repaired and returned to service.

The continued bombing led to the withdrawal of Serbian forces from Kosovo, with hostilities ceasing on June 9, when a peace agreement was reached. The seventy-eight-day war in Kosovo was a much-different war for the A-10 with respect to Operation Desert Storm because of different terrain and weather prevalent in an eastern Europe environment that is engulfed in clouds. A-10 forward air controller aircraft would fly over 1,000 missions during the war.

Approximately fifty to sixty Serbian targets were destroyed by USAF aircraft overall during the war, with the A-10 aircraft one of the weapon systems that attacked Serbian tanks and armored vehicles.

A member of maintenance personnel checks the wing of an A-10 aircraft from the 81st FS, from Spangdahlem, that is participating during Operation Allied Force in Kosovo in 1999.
USAF photo by Senior Airman Jeffrey Allen

An A-10 aircraft with the distinctive black tail fin tips associated with the 81st FS is over Serbia, armed with Maverick missiles. All A-10 aircraft at this time were painted in the two-toned light-gray scheme to allow the aircraft to blend in better with the sky background. *USAF photo by Senior Airman Greg L. Davis*

In addition to the black tail fin tips and the SP tail code, the 81st FS A-10s that participated had black-panther head markings on each engine nacelle. The 81st FS participated both in Operation Deliberate Force in 1994 and Operation Allied Force in 1999. *USAF photo by Senior Airman Greg L. Davis*

This close-up shows the damage that was sustained on the right engine of Major Haun's A-10 aircraft on May 2, 1999, after a missile hit. The aircraft would be repaired and returned to service. *USAF*

Two A-10s from the 81st FS have just completed aerial refueling and are equipped both with bombs and Maverick missiles. *USAF photo by Senior Airman Greg L. Davis*

CHAPTER 10
Operation Enduring Freedom: Afghanistan

The tragic attacks in New York City and Washington, DC, by terrorists on September 11, 2001, would lead to US involvement in Afghanistan (where the terrorists were based), known as Operation Enduring Freedom. Initial attacks were conducted in October 2001 in the form of bombing of targets in Afghanistan both by land-based bombers and carrier-based aircraft and eventually US armed forces.

During the initial invasion of Afghanistan, the A-10 aircraft was not utilized. But by early 2002, as more and more ground support missions evolved, the A-10 was an active part of US forces deployed there. The first such sighting of A-10 aircraft was at Bagram Air Base, where the aircraft supported Operation Anaconda in March 2002.

It was becoming apparent that the A-10 could provide more coverage in the region than what the US helicopters could provide, particularly in the thinner air of the mountainous areas of Afghanistan. The A-10 had better loiter times over target in comparison to the helicopters, which had to keep moving while firing.

With the war reaching over fifteen years in duration by the fall of 2016, there have been many different A-10 units that were deployed to the region, with some squadrons having served multiple tours. The following chart shows the different A-10 squadrons that have participated at some point during Operation Enduring Freedom. Typically, each squadron is assigned for a six-month rotation.

Home Base	Squadron (TFS)	Wing (FW)
Arkansas ANG, Arkansas	188th	
Davis-Monthan AFB, Arizona	354th	355th
Eielson AFB, Alaska	355th	354th
Idaho ANG, Idaho	190th	124th
Martin ANG, Maryland	104th	175th
Moody AFB, Georgia	75th	
New Orleans NAS, Louisiana	706th	926th
Pope AFB, North Carolina	74th and 75th	23rd
Seymour Johnson AFB, North Carolina	366th	
Spangdahlem AB, Germany	81st	52nd
Whiteman AFB, Missouri	303rd	442nd
Willow Grove ANG, Pennsylvania	103rd	111th

The main base for A-10 deployment in the region has been from Bagram Air Base in Afghanistan, with occasional operations from Kandahar Air Base. The war in Afghanistan is significantly different for the A-10 aircraft in comparison to the wars in Iraq and eastern Europe, since there are fewer armored targets such as tanks and artillery to attack; however, more close air support is needed when hostile forces attack US ground troops.

US ground troops who are based in Afghanistan see the A-10 as a morale booster when it flies overhead toward enemy positions. At the same time, enemy forces can see the aircraft as well, and it can provide a significant fear factor when the aircraft does a show-of-force pass followed by a gun-strafing pass, and this was demonstrated in several incidents that required the A-10.

One such operation took place on October 28, 2008, when two A-10 pilots from the 74th Expeditionary Fighter Squadron (EFS), Capt. Parvin and Capt. Cavazos, flew out of Bagram Air Base to a location over 300 miles away to help special-operations Marines in Badhis Province. The two aircraft flew with a dedicated tanker aircraft, and it took over an hour to arrive on-site.

The Marine Special Operations team was on routine patrol 2 miles from a forward operation base when they were attacked by over fifty insurgents. Six Marines became separated from the group and ended up in a house that was attacked. The A-10 aircraft flew over four hours of CAS missions in this region and conducted twenty gun passes that killed the enemy insurgents who were threatening the Marines. It was noted during the debriefing of the operation that the F-18 aircraft that were in the area were not able to fire because of the heavy cloud cover, which the A-10 aircraft were able to penetrate. Both A-10 pilots received Distinguished Flying Cross with Valor medals.

Another event took place in Afghanistan on June 22, 2013. On that day, sixty US army personnel in a convoy that was performing a routine clearance patrol were ambushed by enemy forces. The soldiers were pinned behind their vehicle, and three soldiers sustained injuries that required evacuation and subsequent close air support.

A two-ship deployment of A-10s from the 74th EFS from Moody AFB was sent to the area. An initial show-of-force pass failed to persuade the enemy to voluntarily leave the area. The lead aircraft then marked the enemy position with two marking rockets. This allowed the wingman to come to shoot at the enemy position with the 30 mm gun.

This stirred up even more action from the enemy, and more gun passes from the A-10 were needed. It was still not safe to bring the helicopters to evacuate the wounded personnel. Even after two passes, the large formation of enemy forces was not willing to fall back. In fact, these forces were still advancing and were very close to the US position, and the A-10 aircraft were then authorized to perform a "danger-close" pass, carried out when there was risk to US troops. The A-10 then came in for a low-angle gun pass at 75 feet above enemy position, while being parallel to US forces to avoid any friendly-fire incidents. The A-10 aircraft completed fifteen gun passes, which expended nearly all rounds, as well as dropping three 500-pound bombs. The last pass finally stopped the enemy, and the A-10 remained to provide "Sandy" support for the rescue helicopters.

Attempts made by the USAF to use aircraft such as the B-1 for ground support missions showed the limitation of aircraft that cannot fly low enough to the ground to the point of knowing where forces are located. Indeed, A-10 pilots have the capability to use visual means to clearly identify where the enemy forces are located with respect to friendly forces.

Through 2015, there were no reported losses of A-10 aircraft during Operation Enduring Freedom. In 2015, A-10 aircraft were redeployed from Afghanistan to be based in Turkey to fight ISIS in Iraq and Syria. However, in late 2017, Afghan officials were strongly asking for the return of the A-10 aircraft, which is very unusual for foreign officials to do (i.e., requesting a specific type of aircraft). It is apparent that the A-10 has made its mark in the role of ground support. In January 2018, A-10s from the 303rd EFS from Whiteman AFB, Missouri, were deployed to Kandahar airfield to participate in the campaign to attack drug facilities in Helmond Province. These operations show a turning point where economic targets are considered important tactical targets as well as conventional military targets.

A lone A-10 takes off near the mountains of Afghanistan in December 2008. *USAF photo by SSgt Samuel Morse*

In 2002, the A-10 finally started showing up in force in Afghanistan, supporting Operation Enduring Freedom. The mission for the A-10 was significantly different than in Europe or in Operation Desert Storm, in that there would be no tanks present and, instead, armed outposts would be attacked. Here is an ARES A-10 aircraft from the 706th TFS, part of the 926th FW Cajuns, from the New Orleans Naval Air Station (NAS), which is on the flight line at Bagram Air Base, Afghanistan. *USAF photo by TSgt Melissa Sanscrainte*

Ground crew are conducting engine tests on A-10 aircraft at Bagram Air Base, Afghanistan, in May 2002, with the mountains in the background. The maneuverability of the A-10 aircraft would be a key component in the military operations conducted in the rugged environment of this country. The A-10 was capable of flying into remote areas where other aircraft would not be able to go. *USAF photo by TSgt Melissa Sanscrainte*

Beginning in March 2002, the first group of A-10 aircraft to be deployed to Afghanistan in support of Operation Enduring Freedom would come from the 74th TFS of the 23rd FW, which was at that time based out of Pope AFB in North Carolina. This base supported Operation Anaconda, which took place in March 2002. The 74th TFS aircraft featured the shark's-teeth artwork on the nose, along with the FT tail code. The squadron had served ten years earlier in Operation Desert Storm in Iraq. They were based out of Bagram Air Base until late 2002, when they would be relieved by A-10 units from other US Air Force bases. *USAF photo by SSgt Ricky A. Bloom*

The next group of A-10 aircraft to be deployed into Afghanistan was the Air Force Reserve units that came from the 303rd TFS, based at Whiteman AFB, Missouri, and the 706th FS from the NAS based out of New Orleans, Louisiana. This A-10 aircraft, tail number 79-111, is from the Cajuns from the New Orleans NAS base but was being flown by a pilot from the Whiteman AFRES group. The aircraft from these bases were situated in Bagram from April through July 2002, and they would be replaced by the 75th TFS from Pope AFB. *USAF photo by SSgt Ricky A. Bloom*

The first A-10 ANG squadron to be deployed to Afghanistan was the 104th FW, from Martin ANG base in Maryland, beginning in early 2003. This A-10 is supporting a coalition offensive known as Operation Valiant Strike in March 2003. In this offensive, the A-10s participated in attacks against villages and cave complexes in the area east of Kandahar. The A-10 was being used in a very different role during Operation Enduring Freedom as compared to previous wars, in that there were fewer armored targets to attack but more strategic targets to attack in the rugged terrain of the region, as part of supporting the coalition ground troops. *USAF photo by TSgt Adam Johnston*

The A-10s from the 303rd TFS, out of Whitman AFB in Missouri, did tours in Afghanistan in 2002, 2006, and 2008. Rotations would typically go on a four-to-six-month cycle for the different A-10 units that served in the region, as part of keeping pilots trained in the region as well as keeping fresh pilots in service. The aircraft is painted in the basic gray scheme, which allows it to blend in with the landscape and the sky.
USAF photo by TSgt Francisco V. Govea II

The 355th TFS A-10 unit, based out of Davis-Monthan AFB, Arizona, did a number of tours in Afghanistan during Operation Enduring Freedom. The first deployment of this squadron began in December 2003 and continued into 2004, with additional deployments in 2005, 2006, 2007, and 2009. This A-10 is leaving from Kandahar Air Base for a ground support mission that was conducted in December 2009. The 355th TS is another A-10 group that traces service back to Operation Desert Storm, ten years earlier.
USAF photo by TSgt Francisco V. Govea II

There were many night flights that were conducted with the A-10 aircraft during Operation Enduring Freedom. This A-10 from the 103rd TFS, based out of Willow Grove AFRC, Pennsylvania, is preparing for a night mission in Afghanistan, with the camera using a night vision filter similar to the night vision goggles that the pilot wears. *USAF photo by Airman 1st Class Andrew Oquendo*

These photos were taken of a 23rd FW A-10 after it has conducted aerial refueling over Afghanistan in early 2011. This aircraft features the false-canopy paint scheme on the lower front fuselage, a pattern that was started over thirty-five years previously on the aircraft. The aircraft continues to patrol the region up to the present. *USAF photos by MSgt William Greer*

CHAPTER 11

Operation Iraqi Freedom: Return to Iraq

In 2003, tensions rose again in Iraqi over the possibility that the country had weapons of mass destruction, as well as the fact that Saddam Hussein was still in power. As a result, twelve years after Operation Desert Storm, the US would lead an invasion of allied forces against Iraqi, named Operation Iraqi Freedom, which began on March 20, 2003.

In contrast to Operation Desert Storm, the A-10 was deployed immediately to the region, beginning in early March 2003. Also, instead of being based out of Saudi Arabia, the aircraft was based primarily in Kuwait at the Al Jaber Air Base, as part of the 332nd Air Expeditionary Wing (AEW). Shortly after the war started, another A-10 base that would be used was Prince Hassan Air Base in Jordan, known as the 387th Air Expeditionary Group (AEG).

Official numbers put the number of A-10s deployed from Kuwait at around sixty aircraft, and another eighteen aircraft were deployed from Jordan during the aerial campaign against Iraq that took place in March and April 2003. A-10 aircraft were taken from seven different A-10 bases located in different areas in the United States, as shown in the following table:

A-10s Deployed at Al Jaber AB, Kuwait

332nd AEW (sixty aircraft)

FW	TFS	Home Base Location in US
23rd	74th and 75th	Pope AFB, North Carolina
110th	172nd	Battle Creek ANG, Michigan
111th	103rd	Willow Grove ARS, Pennsylvania
124th	190th	Gowen AFB, Idaho
442nd	202nd	Whiteman AFB, Missouri

A-10s Deployed at Prince Hassan AB, Jordan

387th AEG (eighteen aircraft)

FW	TFS	Home Base Location in US
103rd	118th	Bradley ANG, Connecticut
104th	131st	Barnes ANG, Massachusetts

Invasion points came both from northern and southern Iraq, and the A-10 would support ground troops from both directions. Later, as more parts of Iraq were captured, A-10s would be based from forward bases such as Tallil Air Base in Nasiriyah, Iraq, about 220 miles southeast of Baghdad, and Kirkuk Air Base, in northern Iraq.

There was only one A-10 aircraft that was lost during the war. This happened on April 8, when A-10, tail number 78-0691, with the 190th TFS from Idaho was shot down by an Iraqi Roland SAM near Baghdad International Airport. Fortunately, the pilot survived and was rescued.

A few other A-10s received damage, either in the form of missiles or ground fire. One A-10, tail number 80-0258, from the 172nd TFS from the Battle Creek ANG group, received a hit in the right engine from a shoulder-mounted SAM missile. The aircraft was able to be flown back to base by the pilot, and the aircraft was then repaired to flying status to return to the US.

Perhaps the most notable A-10 incident during the war occurred one day earlier, on April 7, when the A-10, tail number 81-0897, flown by Capt. Kim Campbell, flying for the 75th FS from Pope AFB in North Carolina, was hit by ground fire near Baghdad. Campbell was providing support to US ground troops in the Baghdad area when her aircraft was hit with enemy fire. The aircraft sustained damage to the tail section and the hydraulic system. Despite the significant amount of damage, Campbell was able to land the aircraft back at base.

The aerial campaign ran from March 20 through May 1, a period of time that was similar in length to Operation Desert Storm. There were a total of sixty A-10 aircraft that were deployed as part of Operation Iraqi Freedom. Over 311,000 rounds of 30 mm shells were expended by the A-10 during the first phase of the war, along with over 900 Maverick missiles being fired.

In comparison to Operation Desert Storm, there were fewer A-10 aircraft that were deployed to the region this time around.

Part of this reduction had to do with the fact that there were a number of A-10 aircraft being used in Afghanistan at the time, supporting ground troops in the other war involving the US.

The A-10 also flew thirty-two leaflet missions as part of PSYOPS, along with the F-16, F-18, and B-52. With regard to the effectiveness of the A-10 and other aircraft against Iraqi armor, statistics were not as precise as were those that were collected during Operation Desert Storm. However, the number of tanks that were still in Iraq in 2003 (which was under 2,000) were either destroyed by allied forces or junked shortly after the war.

Withdrawal of many of the A-10 units began in December 2003. However, it would not be long before the aircraft's presence was needed again in the country to deal with the resulting insurgency after the fall of the Hussein government. In late 2006, A-10 aircraft were deployed to Al Asad Airfield, Iraq; Air Combat Command (ACC) activated the 438th Air as part of the 438th AEG.

In 2007, the first A-10C model made its appearance in Iraq, with the deployment of aircraft from the 131st TFS of the Maryland ANG from Martin Air Force Base. A-10s from other US bases would continue to be deployed in the region as required. With the advent of ISIS (Islamic State of Iraq and Syria), various ground targets would require the return of the A-10 to the region.

This would be the last war in which there was a mass of opposing tanks that the A-10 was deployed against. Tanks in an open-landscape environment have been proven to be tactically useless when airpower is involved. Wars of the future will have smaller numbers of tanks for the A-10 to attack, and thus it will be engaging soft positions such as enemy positions that may have gun setups and artillery. The days of conventional warfare with massive amounts of equipment to be attacked are ending, and the newer types of mission where there are precision attacks on specific targets by the A-10, both in urban and rural terrain, are becoming increasingly common.

A-10 aircraft of the 111th FW from the Willow Grove ARS taxi to their parking spaces, at a forward-deployed location in southern Iraq in March 2003, in support of Operation Iraqi Freedom. *USAF photo by Shane Cuomo*

A-10 aircraft from the 74th TFS takes off from Tallil AB for a mission on March 29, with the Iraqi sun in the background. *USAF photo by Senior Airman JoAnn S. Makinano*

A-10s from the 442nd FW prepare for takeoff to go to Tallil Air Base in April 2003. *USAF photo by MSgt Terry L. Bevins*

A-10 from the Willow Grove ARS prepares for taking off on a mission in Iraq during April 2003. *USAF photo by SSgt Shane Cuomo*

Ground crew are working on getting 442nd FW A-10 ready for its next mission. *USAF photo by SSgt Lee A Osberry*

A-10 from 23rd FW is being serviced at a forward base in March 2003. Paint has peeled off in areas around the cannon, indicating probable impact damage that was incurred during aerial refueling. *USAF photo by Senior Airman JoAnn S. Makinano*

A pair of A-10s from the Pope AFB group (23rd FW) are preparing for takeoff in a mission. *USAF photo by Captain Ken Hill*

A-10 from 74th TFS in September 2003 drops a flare to deflect any heat-seeking missiles in action near Kirkuk in northern Iraq. *USAF photo by SSgt James A. Williams*

A-10 from the 110th FW from Battle Creek received a hit in April 2003 from a SAM missile. It was repaired and returned to service. *USAF photo by SSgt Shane Cuomo*

Technician is repairing some of the many holes caused by ground fire on an A-10 with tail number 81-0987, flown by Capt. Kim Campbell. *USAF photo by MSgt Stephan Alford*

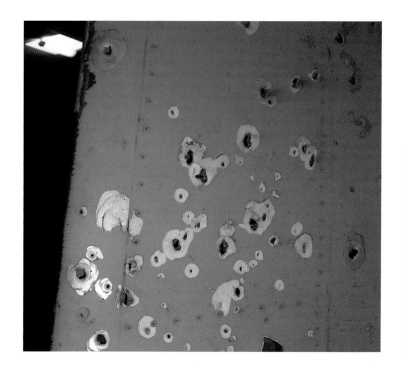

The horizontal stabilizers from 81-0987 were beyond repair, and one stabilizer was donated to the Cradle of Aviation museum on Long Island. *Ken Neubeck*

The damaged fuselage section of 81-0987 was deemed too expensive to repair, and it was shipped back to the US for teardown and inspection to certify the A-10 fleet. *USAF*

This A-10 is being refueled and armed for a mission in Iraq in March 2003. It has conventional bombs, along with two Maverick missiles and a rocket launcher under its left wing for marking targets. There were some A-10 aircraft that were also deployed in Afghanistan at the same time as the war in Iraq, which made for a higher workload for the aircraft, pilots, and ground crew for the A-10 fleet. *USAF photo by SSgt Shane Cuomo*

Five A-10s from the 303rd Tactical Fighter Squadron, 442nd Fighter Wing, based at Whiteman Air Force Base, Missouri, are being prepped for an upcoming mission during Operation Iraqi Freedom in April 2003. In contrast to Operation Desert Storm, when over 150 A-10 aircraft were deployed in the region, Operation Iraqi Freedom saw less than half that number of A-10s deployed, a total of sixty aircraft for the war effort. *USAF photo by Captain Ken Hill*

A-10 from the 74th TFS in flight over Iraq in June 2003 is armed with Maverick missiles and bombs. The 74th TFS also participated in Operation Desert Storm in 1991 and made a return to the region for this war. Although the main air campaign for Operation Iraqi Freedom ended on May 1, the A-10s deployed there would remain in Iraq for the balance of 2003 in order to carry on various support missions. *USAF photo by SSgt Lee A. Osberry*

A-10s from the five major A-10 fighter squadrons that participated in the Operation Iraqi Freedom perform a group pass over Ahmed Al Jaber Air Base in Kuwait in late 2003, a few months after the end of the main combat phase. From the top to bottom are A-10 aircraft from the 303rd TFS, out of Whiteman AFB, Missouri (tail code KC); the 103rd TFS, from Willow Grove AFB, Pennsylvania (tail code PA); the 172nd TFS, from Battle Creek, Michigan (tail code BC); the 190th TFS, from Gowen Field, Idaho (tail code ID); and the 75th TFS, from Pope AFB, North Carolina (tail code FT). *USAF*

A-10 from the 74th TFS in December 2003 is leaving for the US from Tallil Air Base. *USAF photo by SSgt Chenzira Mallory*

When US forces returned to Iraq again, the A-10C version made its combat debut in Iraq with this aircraft from the 131st TFS in October 2007. *USAF photo by SSgt Angelique Perez*

CHAPTER 12
Operation Odyssey Dawn: Libya

In March 2011, NATO initiated Operation Odyssey Dawn to prevent the slaughter of Libyan rebels by the government forces of Col. Qaddafi. By the end of March, the US deployed a number of aircraft to complement the NATO air forces of France and Britain. Part of this deployment included six A-10C aircraft that were from the 81st FW, which had been based at Spangdahlem airbase in Germany and had moved to Aviano airbase in Italy.

A significant number of ground targets such as government armored vehicles and trucks were destroyed by allied aircraft during enforcement of the no-fly zone over Libya. A-10C aircraft were working with AC-130 gunships as early as March 25 in ground attacks.

On March 29, an A-10C aircraft accompanied a P-3C Orion aircraft in response to ships of the Libyan coast guard firing indiscriminately at merchant vessels at the port of Misrata, in the northwestern portion of Libya. The P-3C attacked the patrol vessel *Vittoria* with missiles, which damaged it to the point of being beached. The A-10 aircraft used the 30 mm cannon to attack two smaller Libyan crafts, destroying one and forcing the other to be abandoned. This maritime role for the A-10 was a mission that was once anticipated by Fairchild Republic back in 1980, in one of their foreign sales presentations.

By the first week of April, US involvement in Libya was reduced strictly to the support role, and this meant the withdrawal of the A-10 at that time from Libya operations. This withdrawal actually made more news than actual A-10 combat action, because there were no other NATO aircraft that were capable of flying at a low enough altitude so that they could discriminate between the pro-Qaddafi forces and the rebels. The US maintained that the A-10s were available if NATO requested them, but no further action would ensure that required the participation of the Warthog.

The action in Libya, along with other military actions that have occurred, shows the importance of the A-10 base being located in Spangdahlem at the time. From this central location, the aircraft was able to be deployed to forward bases at other European locations such as Italy or Sicily for action in northern Africa, eastern Europe, the Middle East, and, of course, Afghanistan.

A-10 Warthog, tail number 82-0656, is returning to Spangdahlem Air Base in Germany in April 2011 after being deployed to Libya as part of a six-aircraft contingent of A-10s to support NATO operations. *Niels Roman*

CHAPTER 13
Operation Inherent Resolve: Syria

After the US withdrawal from Iraq in 2013, changes in the region occurred in the northern region of Iraq and parts of Syria with the influx of ISIS. This created an upstate political situation in this region, and ISIS took over several oil reserves in the regions

In November 2014, it was announced that several A-10s from the 163rd Fighter Squadron of the Indiana Air National Guard that were deployed to Afghanistan were now being deployed to Kuwait to support Operation Inherent Resolve, to focus on the fight against ISIS. This action may have been the result of meetings with coalition forces and a realization that with fewer ground targets being hit by other aircraft in the coalition, smaller tactical targets needed to be addressed by an aircraft such as the A-10.

At one point, it became apparent that this situation had to be dealt with. In mid-2015, A-10C aircraft were deployed to an airbase at Incilrik, Turkey. From there, the A-10 could fly to areas in northern Iraq and parts of Syria where ISIS was operating.

Major actions would soon begin in the fall of 2015. In early November 2015, Operation Tidal Wave II began when four A-10C aircraft, along with two AC-130 gunships, were deployed to the Deir ez-Zor region in eastern Syria, near the border of Iraq. It was there that they encountered hundreds of oil trucks that were in the process of transporting oil from the oil production facilities in this region.

The aircraft dropped warning leaflets prior to the attack to warn drivers and civilians that parked trucks would be targeted. Once this was done, the aircraft attacked all oil trucks in the area, with over 116 trucks being damaged or destroyed. By targeting these trucks, it adversely affected the economic lifeline to ISIS.

A subsequent attack with A-10C and AC-130 aircraft took place two weeks later in the same region. Again, warnings were given prior to the attack, and then 280 oil trucks were destroyed. Another strike took place in August 2016, in which eighty-three oil trucks in the same region were destroyed by A-10 and F-16 aircraft. These and smaller attacks destroyed over 600 oil trucks, thus having a further impact on ISIS.

A-10 Operations in Syria continued through 2017, up through late 2018.

View of this A-10 Warthog in Operation Inherent Resolve shows some of the weapons mounted on stations of the aircraft. The telltale sign of gun residue from 30 mm cannon use can be seen on the lower fuselage, engine nacelles, and tail section. *USAF photo via SSgt Trevor McBride*

Battle-worn A-10 Warthog based in Turkey, participating in Operation Inherent Resolve, in July 2017, shows the heavy usage that this particular aircraft has seen. The paint is worn away around the USARSI refueling port, and there are dents on the nose of the fuselage, indicative of multiple aerial refuelings for this aircraft. *USAF photo via SSgt Trevor McBride*

A-10C Warthog has just refueled in the area near Turkey that is participating in Operation Inherent Resolve, where the A-10 was used to attack ISIS targets in Iraq and Syria, in May 2017.
USAF photo via SSgt Michael Battles

CHAPTER 14
Deployment to Eastern Europe

From 2015 through 2017, A-10s from different squadrons were deployed to different countries in eastern Europe as sort of a show of force toward Russia. This involved the rotation of a few A-10 units, typically four to twelve aircraft staying for a month to participate in joint exercises with the host country's armed forces.

It is ironic that many of the countries that were visited were former members of the Warsaw Pact, which had the large tank forces during the 1980s that the A-10 was designed to counteract. It is almost inconceivable to see such a change in the political climate over the course of only thirty years.

Date	Country	Squadron	Operation
March 2015	Romania	354th	Op. Atlantic Resolve
May 2015	Slovakia	104th	Op. Atlantic Resolve
May 2015	Bulgaria	354th	Op. Atlantic Resolve
May 2015	Estonia	354th	Op. Atlantic Resolve
June 2015	Poland	354th	Op. Atlantic Resolve
August 2015	Czech	23rd	Op. Atlantic Resolve
August 2015	Romania	366th	Op. Atlantic Resolve
September 2015	Estonia	303rd	Op. Atlantic Resolve
December 2015	Hungary	354th	Op. Atlantic Resolve
June 2016	Estonia	354th	Op. Saber Strike
July 2016	Slovakia	122nd	Op. Atlantic Resolve
August 2017	Estonia	354th	Op. Atlantic Resolve

A-10C aircraft from the 354th EFS is visiting Papa Air Base in Hungary in December 2015 as part of the Theater Security Package (TSP) portion of Operation Atlantic Resolve. *USAF photo by Capt. Lauren Ott*

A-10C from the 104th FS is landing and taking off from Jagala Karavete highway in Estonia as part of
Operation Atlantic Resolve in August 2017. *USAF photo by Senior Airman Ryan Conroy*

Two US combat controllers are guiding an A-10 that was deployed from the 104th FS in MD to Estonia as part of Operation Atlantic Resolve in August 2017. *USAF photo by Senior Airman Ryan Conroy*

It seems that the political wars to retain the A-10 aircraft in the US inventory have been far greater than the actual wars that the aircraft has participated in. Indeed, for a good part of the new millennium, the future of the A-10 has been the subject of much debate between Congress and the Air Force.

Beginning in 2013, anticipated budget cuts led the USAF to propose retiring the A-10, and for the next two years, on a weekly basis, there was a lot of intense discussion between Congress and the Pentagon regarding the future of the A-10. The Air Force has cited the need to eliminate the A-10 from the inventory to be able to save money, as well as the stated need for A-10 maintainers to transition to the new F-35 aircraft.

However, the A-10 aircraft has had several proponents in Congress, some of whom served on the Senate Armed Services Committee. These senators have a lot of firsthand knowledge on the aircraft; for example, former New Hampshire senator Kelly Ayotte's husband was a former A-10 pilot, and former Navy pilot John McCain (1936–2018) represented the state of Arizona, which has Davis-Monthan AFB, with its A-10s. In addition, a lot of firsthand accounts from Army personnel who served in Afghanistan have been used as supporting evidence to save the aircraft.

The crux of the discussion, besides the two sides, is whether other aircraft such as the F-16, F-18, and B-1 can provide effective CAS support for the US Army and US Marines in different theaters. But there have been many examples in the combat zones that the A-10 is the only aircraft capable of real CAS and is the only one that can go "danger close" and not hurt friendly forces.

By the beginning of 2017, with a new administration, the efforts toward retiring the A-10 had ceased, and the A-10 now is to remain active until 2030 to deal with sustained conflicts. However, the one enemy that is now an issue for the A-10 is Father Time. The last A-10, built in 1984, is over thirty-five years old,

and with 12,000 flying hours being the general lifetime limit for the airframe, it can be seen that there will be challenges in keeping the A-10 in the fleet.

As of June 2017, there were 283 A-10 aircraft that were still active in the US inventory. However, about ninety of these A-10s need rewinging to allow them to stay in service, and a budget and a contractor are needed for this work. In the meantime, with two active theaters of conflict in Afghanistan and the Middle East, the Air Force has used the process of rotation of A-10 aircraft, typically on a six-month basis to spread the accumulation of flying hours.

There are moves to supplement the A-10's role in CAS with light attack aircraft that already exist. This makes sense in regard to allocating mission tasks and extending the life of the remaining A-10 aircraft. The process of starting a new aircraft program from scratch to replace the A-10 would be a long process and would take several years.

The A-10 is being considered for special use in civilian agencies such as the National Science Foundation for hurricane chasing. Even if the A-10 is retired, it is conceivable that the aircraft could be run by museum organizations under strict control.

In the meantime, there will be a number of A-10s that will be required for the different theaters of war that the US continues to be involved with. There is a plan as mandated by Congress in the fiscal year 2017 National Defense Authorization Act for head-to-head comparison tests between the A-10 Warthog and the F-35 Lighting II to see which aircraft will be best suited for the CAS mission going forward. Part of the consideration is that the F-35, which has less ammunition than the A-10, would have an attachable gun pod added to its lower fuselage, but the vibration aspects on this aircraft still have to be determined, as well as how the addition of such a gun pod would affect accuracy. The controversy regarding the A-10 continues.

A-10, tail number 78-0621, from the Connecticut ANG, is visiting MacDill AFB and has a special World War II "Black Lightning" paint scheme in honor of the eightieth anniversary of the unit. *John Gourley*

In 2017, the National Science Foundation (NSF) received a retired A-10 (tail number 80-0212) from Davis-Monthan AFB, to be equipped with meteorological equipment along with armoring and deicing capability to adapt this aircraft for storm-chasing tasks for tracking tornadoes in "Tornado Alley" in the US. *Bob Bluth, Naval Postgraduate School*

Early-morning photo shows a pair of A-10 Warthogs from the Maryland AFB during a November 2015 visit to Republic Airport on Long Island. *Ken Neubeck*